EMPOWERED TO CARE

PASTORAL CARE IN THE CHURCH

EMPOWERED TO CARE

PASTORAL CARE IN THE CHURCH

 **PASTORAL CARE OFFICE**

COPYRIGHT © 1980
Herald Publishing House
Independence, Missouri

All rights in this book are reserved. No part of the text may be reproduced in any form without written permission of the publisher, except brief quotations used in connection with reviews in magazines or newspapers.

Printed in the United States of America

CONTENTS

FOREWORD 7

PREFACE 9

PASTORAL CARE
   by Harry J. Ashenhurst 11

PASTORAL CARE AND THE GROWTH OF PERSONS
   by Kay Sheridan 32

THE UNIQUENESS OF PASTORAL CARE
   by Joe A. Serig 55

PASTORAL CARE: MEETING HUMAN NEEDS
   by S. Lee Pfohl   67

CARING IN THE FAMILY
   by Irene Jones 87

PLANNING FOR COMPREHENSIVE CARE
   by Pat Zahniser 102

ISSUES IN PASTORAL CARE
   by Myron Andes, Jr. 129

PASTORAL CARE AND PRIESTHOOD
   RESPONSIBILITY
   by A. Bruce Lindgren.....................153

PASTORAL CARE AND COUNSELING
   by R. Daniel Fenn 169

PASTORAL CARE ACTIVITIES
   by Carol Anderson Anway..................188

AUTHORS 219

FOREWORD

As we enter a new decade for the church with the Faith to Grow program drawing us forward, we are excited about the possibilities facing our church members. Avenues of ministry are going to be opening up all around us in the 1980s, and we have faith that our people will respond in caring and prophetic ways.

Empowered to Care will be a helpful resource to congregations and individual church members. Caring is the foundation of the Faith to Grow program. This resource provides a variety of chapters dealing with different aspects of caring in congregational life. We recommend its diligent study, and pray that many of the concepts and practical ideas it mentions will find concrete expression in your Christian life-style.

> THE FIRST PRESIDENCY

PREFACE

The Pastoral Care Office is pleased to present this resource to the church. It is the first book made available by the church which provides a comprehensive statement concerning pastoral care. We believe the articles give helpful information to all people interested in creating caring life-styles, e.g. administrators, congregational leaders, priesthood, parents, members in general, and friends of the church.

Empowered to Care is available because of the hard work of many people. We would like to thank the authors who contributed chapters to this book; Lee Pfohl and Myron Andes, Jr., for their diligent planning in the early stages of production; and R. Daniel Fenn who edited the resource through to its completion.

We pray that the church will benefit from the information contained here. It is our desire that all people will eventually see the need for pastoral care ministry. May God bless you as you endeavor to develop personal and congregational caring life-styles.

Pastoral Care Office

PASTORAL CARE
by Harry J. Ashenhurst

As I drove up to the small weather-beaten church I began to wonder what the people would be like. Getting out of the car I realized I was early and alone, giving me an opportunity to look around. What I saw was a quiet rural town, tucked away from any main highways, cozily asleep on a fall Saturday morning. The image of a town struggling for survival emerged strongly in my mind. I could not help wondering whether this little church community was also fighting for its life.

The greetings from the Saints as they arrived were warm and friendly—typical of RLDS congregations. Yet there was a different look in their eyes, a mixture of fear and anger. Strange, I thought. I was here to do a two-day congregational planning workshop. Why would people be angry or fearful about setting goals and objectives?

I didn't have to wait long to find out. Before the workshop even began two people approached me quietly to "warn" me of certain individuals who would probably cause trouble. Sure enough. One hour into our workshop there was trouble. But it didn't come just from those I had been warned about. And it didn't have anything to do with goals and objectives. The problem was people. People who were angry at each other. People who were hurt and in pain. People who lashed out aggressively in blindness. People who had a basic fear about where they were going and what was happening to their lives.

The needs of this group did not point to a need for establishing goals and objectives. The needs were reconciliation, healing, and a basic caring for each other. Somewhere in their life together they had become separated and alienated, and had lost a sensitivity to each other's human need. Regardless of the cause, the result was a community divided and broken in their relationships. They appeared unwilling to forgive and heal.

In such a situation what kind of ministry is required? What facet of our Christian calling is needed? Where do we begin to offer help? How is a community motivated to move from brokenness to wholeness? These questions are difficult, not easily answered, and not unique to this small rural congregation.

NATURE OF THE HUMAN CONDITION

Human suffering knows no partiality. It invades the lives of all people, regardless of economic status, religious beliefs, and spiritual maturity. Brokenness is part of life. Separateness is part of life. To understand that we are individuals, distinct from all other individuals and thus separate, is to understand part of the meaning of life. To attempt to ignore our brokenness and separateness is to ignore a given in life. Too often the impression is shared that wholeness is synonymous with completeness, that as humans it is possible to achieve a state of total wholeness. People live by the hope and gain meaning from the idea that wholeness connotes total absence of brokenness. The subtle implication is that wholeness, devoid of brokenness, is somehow humanly attainable. Even though wholeness is also recognized as a growing process the human tendency is to want something that is eventually complete and total.

When we look at our human condition it may be more helpful to view brokenness and wholeness in a *dialectic* relationship. That is, when you reflect on one you cannot help but reflect on the other. Neither is a total way of *being* in the world—both are parts of our lives and are experienced together in process. They are human experiences in continuing opposition. One totally without the other is not possible.

Brokenness and wholeness are present realities in life. Recognizing brokenness as a given is not the same as giving it equal value with wholeness. Brokenness is not to be celebrated simply for its own sake. Yet it is not to be ignored in its value as a tool in living a life of wholeness.

The people in our small rural congregation were being dominated and controlled by their brokenness. It had become so strong that their sense of wholeness with the self and each other was lost. Their lives together had become entangled in a process of hurt, pain, and rejection. No longer could they use their brokenness as a way of confession and sharing, thus generating a sense of healing and wholeness. Instead, brokenness was the end in itself, and the lives of these people were being permanently damaged.

This congregation could find hope in using their brokenness as a way of growing and maturing. Hurt and rejection could show them the meaning and possibility of happiness and acceptance. When they experience and understand pain they can come to the realization of its alternative—joy. When people can experience their brokenness and reflect on its meaning and potential learning value then brokenness becomes a tool for wholeness. The point is not to be overcome by brokenness but to share it, reflect upon it, confess it, and use it as a healing process.

The *push* of the gospel of Jesus Christ is to reach out and meet the *pull* of the human condition. It is in this interaction of the push and pull that we are called to give care and offer healing. Pastoral care arises out of this pushing of the gospel and the pulling of human need. It becomes a foundation for our ministry. It calls us to seriously reflect on life's brokenness and how to use it creatively in moving people to a process of change and growth. Our small rural congregation needed the ministry of pastoral care as a way of releasing the control of brokenness in their lives, freeing them to forgive, heal, and move toward wholeness.

NATURE AND DEFINITION OF PASTORAL CARE

Pastoral care is a ministry that cuts across all facets of Christian ministry. As C. W. Brister notes, "Pastoral care is the mutual concern of Christians for each other and for those in the world for whom Christ died."[1] Pastoral care is comprehensive by the way it permeates every congregational function, laying the foundation for the ministries of worship, Christian education, stewardship, leadership, evangelism, and Zionic relationships. Pastoral care is specific in the way it calls us to reconciliation, healing, and wholeness—individually and corporately.

The basic affirmation of pastoral care is God's love for every human being. This love is made specific, alive and concrete, as the needs of humanity are brought together with the gospel of Jesus Christ. Through this interaction pastoral care emerges and is lived out.

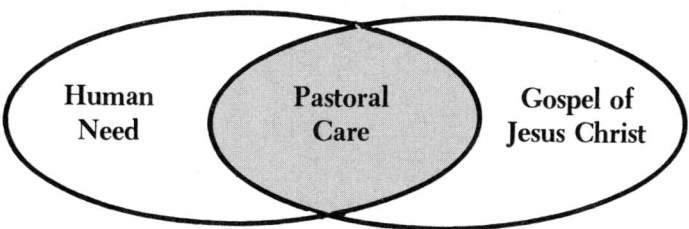

People express a sensitivity to the needs of their fellow human beings. Such care and concern are based on God's love for all persons. Being loved by God prompts us, enables and motivates us, to love and care for those around us. We are moved to confess and share our brokenness together, in the presence of God, and thus learn how to use our brokenness creatively as part of our growing process toward wholeness.

Pastoral care is a process of learning how to understand and be aware of human need and how to respond to that need so that God's reconciling love and healing are felt and experienced. The task is one of response to the wonder of God's care for every individual, sharing this healing power that is available to all. The New Testament, with its witness to the incarnation of God's love, stands as a witness of irrepressible caring concern. In the life of Jesus the Christ we find the basic affirmation of God's love for humanity. As the apostle Paul affirmed,

> Have this mind among yourselves, which is yours in Christ Jesus, who, though he was in the form of God, did not count equality with God a thing to be grasped, but emptied himself, taking the form of a servant, being born in the likeness of man. And being found in human form he humbled himself and became obedient unto death, even death on a cross.—Philippians 2:5-8, Revised Standard Version.

The ministry of pastoral care is to people, not organizations, structures, or programs. We live in a society where institutions do not always serve and affirm people. The caring function never loses sight of its basic calling—the sustaining and enriching of human life with all its value and dignity. Pastoral care embraces the brokenness of life, transforming the potential destructiveness of brokenness into a creative force for healing and wholeness. In its ultimate sense pastoral care frees us to become more fully who we are and can become as the people of God.

PRINCIPLES OF PASTORAL CARE

The uniqueness of pastoral care is expressed in the fact that it lays the foundation for all other facets of Christian ministry. Pastoral care is lived out in all of life's relationships—individual and community. It provides the environment in which the message and ministry of Jesus Christ come alive in people. As such, pastoral care brings together a unique combination of gospel principles, forming the foundation and implementing framework for ministry. A look at these foundational and implementing principles will give a better understanding of pastoral care.

FOUNDATIONAL PRINCIPLES

*1. **Pastoral care is a ministry of** love.* The basic call for pastoral care and Christian ministry is to live a life of love. The scriptures resound with the message of love (e.g. I John 4:16, John 3:16) as the all-pervading action of those claimed by the living Christ. To express love to one's neighbor is to express love for the ultimate power of the universe. To express love to a person lost in pessimism and despair is to live pastoral care.

Love is not finally meaningful in its verbal affirmation but in its action—the doing of love. Some often call the action of love the "impossible possibility" given the complexity and multiplicity of values in modern-day society. The lived out expression of love is not always an easy task. The call for love is heard, yet the action of love is difficult to live. It requires us to reach out to the unlovable—those different from us and those who express no love in return.

It is Erich Fromm[2] who helps us understand that love is an *active power*—a power that breaks through the walls which separate us, uniting us together. Love overcomes our sense of isolation and separateness, yet permits us to be ourselves. "In love the paradox occurs that two beings become one and yet remain two."

Love implies care, trust, patience, respect, and constancy. A parent's love for a child is expressed in every way the parent relates to the child. As the parent provides a stable and constant environment the child experiences love. To love is to show an active concern for the growth of that which is loved. Love precedes all other action. Love permeates all other action. Love is the basis for all of pastoral care. Without the expression of love, pastoral care has no meaning or basis for life.

2. *Pastoral care is a ministry of* healing. The ministry of healing is indeed a comprehensive process involving much more than a physical event. Healing involves all the aspects of one's life—spiritual, emotional, and physical. Within the New Testament the idea of healing is closely related to wholeness—each pointing to the integration of life's purpose and meaning with God. And yet in the same manner as wholeness, healing is often viewed as a process where the pain, loneliness, and sickness in life are totally removed. But the healing process is not devoid of pain or suffering. Healing occurs in the midst of human suffering. To be healed is to recognize and experience suffering as part of growth and not the source of despair. To be healed is to share deeply our pain together to the point where it no longer controls our destiny but becomes part of our creative movement toward wholeness. To be healed is to experience God's love as a way of sharing with us in our humanity—with all its wounds and frailties.

When a wife loses her husband in death the feelings of pain and suffering are very real. The life together of two loving people has been broken—the wound is deep. The ministry of healing does not take away this pain; it shares it. The pain is felt deeply and shared deeply. Healing occurs in the process of sharing the pain. The woman comes to realize the pain as part of who she is and a part of all humanity. God's love in that pain is an act of sharing, giving full value to the presence of pain and yet not allowing it to control her life, but informing her of who she is and can become.

To live a life where healing is freely given is to share in the hurts and wounds of people. The healer and the healed understand the pain of life as something shared and made meaningful in the presence of God's love. Pastoral care calls us all to be the healers and the healed of this world.

3. *Pastoral care is a ministry of* reconciliation. It is the apostle Paul who brings the challenging call of reconciliation to all of humanity.

> **When anyone is united to Christ, there is a new world; the old order has gone, and a new order has already begun. From first to last this has been the work of God. He has reconciled us men to himself**

through Christ, and he has enlisted us in this service of reconciliation. What I mean is, that God was in Christ reconciling the world to himself, no longer holding men's misdeeds against them, and that he has entrusted us with the message of reconciliation—II Corinthians 5:17-19, New English Bible.

Reconciliation takes place in an environment of a caring community. It is the bringing together of that which was separated or lost. Losing a sense of who we are is a frequent experience. Becoming separate from other people by not knowing what is going on in their lives is commonplace. We separate ourselves from God by becoming rigid and narrow-minded in viewing how God calls us to be disciples in this world. Reconciliation is a process of reuniting us to self, others, and God.

The personal expression of forgiveness and acceptance creates the environment for reconciliation. A friend's forgiveness and acceptance of your behavior gives birth to reconciliation. Your forgiveness and acceptance of one who has hurt you produces opportunity for reconciliation. God's forgiveness and acceptance of us all and our willingness to receive this gift of grace bring reconciliation. It is a continual process: separation is part of life and reconciliation is always attempting to break through and reunite that which is broken.

We are to be ambassadors of reconciliation. Our ministry of pastoral care is to create a quality of relationships where the Holy Spirit manifests itself as a powerful force for reconciliation. We experience grace and reconciliation in personal ways as we are willing to give ourselves in sharing the message of God's love and care.

4. *Pastoral care is a ministry of* nurture. Part of being human is to question our own worth and meaning. How often do we doubt our personal value and purpose in living? Given the uncertainties and ambiguities in today's world it would be easy and perhaps even enticing to proclaim a life of despair and gloom.

To question the meaning, purpose, and worth in life is a natural process of being human. The ministry of nurturing one another at the point of our questioning is an act of sustaining and supporting each other in time of personal search. The nurturing process sustains us as we struggle with our humanity and its meaning and purpose. Nurturing and sustaining do not take away the questions and doubts. To nurture means to add a new dimension to our search for meaning—the dimension of acceptance and support in our human struggle. To nurture is to encourage people to search for meaning and purpose. To nurture is to sustain people in times of despair. To nurture is to encourage growth. To nurture is to enter *into* the suffering of our fellow human beings and be *with* them in their personal doubts and pains. To nurture is to affirm God's ultimate love for all persons, regardless of who or where they are.

The ministry of nuture encourages us to explore ourselves and our relationship to others and God. It can be an exciting process where we look at the world in fresh and new ways, affirming the value of wonder and awe in the kaleidoscope of life. A person who is nurtured and sustained has the power to *question* and *affirm* the totality of life. Pastoral care nurtures people, enticing them to grow and mature in the continuing search for meaning and purpose.

5. *Pastoral care is a ministry of* courage. To care for another human being can be a risk-taking event. Caring is a dangerous process because it opens us up to hurt, pain, and possible rejection. Caring moves us into the unknown of another human life where the future is uncertain. The threat of losing the self to or in someone else is real and present.

The courage to care involves a security with yourself to the point where you can enter into the suffering of another person. Courage implies a strong enough sense of self to give of that self in a caring relationship. The risks are always present. We can protect ourselves through indifference or detachment when the risks become too great. But the call to care is to have the courage to risk.

Each of us carries masks of protection from being hurt. We have built these walls of separation through experiences of being rejected and wounded. Involvement can mean pain. The courage to break down these walls and masks of protection comes from a sense of God's final and ultimate involvement in each of our lives. God's involvement in human life, through the witness of Jesus Christ, is the model of courage that risks to care. The courage to care overcomes detachment and indifference. The courage to care brings involvement. The courage to care takes us beyond ourselves into the unknown with the ultimate trust that in this risk we come to truly understand the meaning and purpose in life.

6. *Pastoral care is a ministry of* hope. Through caring comes a sense of hope, a sense of the possibilities that can be realized in another human life. Hope stimulates us to make the possibilities come alive and become reality. In the act of caring one is instilled with a hope for the present and the future. The present comes alive with new growth and a fresh perspective on one's current life situation. The future is viewed as full of significant life options and meaningful relationships. Hope frees us to enter the unknown future with the promise of new life.

To the lives of despair and pain pastoral care brings a ministry of hope. Persons are shown new possibilities for the present and are motivated to courageously move into the future. The divorcee who is lonely and afraid gains the courage to reach out again. The child who has been abused finds new love and care. The youth who is contemplating suicide is given a fresh perspective on life's possibilities. The alcoholic realizes that life can be different and changes can be made. And the healer, who is so often rejected, gains the strength to continue in the fight to bring wholeness out of brokenness. It is hope that makes pastoral care the ministry that prevails over human despair and suffering.

IMPLEMENTING PRINCIPLES

The foundational principles of pastoral care must somehow be brought together in a ministry that people not only hear but experience and live. It is the combining of these principles and their implementation into human life that make pastoral care alive and meaningful. To implement these foundational principles we need to be aware of four other principles that influence how pastoral care is lived out.

1. Pastoral care involves **all persons.** Pastoral care is best understood as a life-style that is lived by every disciple of Christ. Regardless of age or sex every person is called to share the ministry of care and love. A small boy can bring a ministry of pastoral care by simply touching an elderly woman and saying how much he loves her. A teen-age girl expresses care to a five-year-old girl by setting her on her lap and reading a story. The woman who shares in the sadness and rejection of another woman's divorce is living a life-style of pastoral care. Only when pastoral care becomes the ministry of *all* does it become the foundation of Christian ministry.

2. Pastoral care is a continuing **process.** Recognizing pastoral care as a process rather than a specific event does two things for us. First, it helps us realize that a caring ministry is always growing—never stops—and is constantly present in our lives. And second, it focuses pastoral care on the present needs of people, not their needs two months from now. People in need require care and loving concern now. A caring ministry is impossible if it is always postponed to the future, ignoring the present moment of need. To see pastoral care as a process is to look at ministry as a growing, present concern in our midst.

3. Pastoral care involves **community.** There is a corporate or mutual concern involved in a ministry of pastoral care. Caring ministry recognizes the interrelatedness of our lives together and builds upon the potential strength that comes from community effort. Although pastoral care can be and is expressed individually an added power comes to a caring ministry in its corporate sharing. Another way of saying pastoral care is congregational care. The people of God, both gathered and scattered, form the community through which love and care are shared and experienced. In the same way a person lives pastoral care the congregation lives a life-style of care.

4. Pastoral care is **all pervasive.** The ministry of pastoral care penetrates all other forms of ministry. It is important to recognize how all the parts of our ministry involve a basic love and concern for every person. Without this care it is difficult, if not impossible, to teach, worship, or evangelize. The caring concern is the *first and the continuing central* function of ministry for both the individual disciple and the community.

FAITH TO GROW

The church is moving into a new decade with an emphasis on our *Faith to Grow*. The growth process involves both an internal evaluation of who we are and who we want to become and an external evaluation of how we can expand the community of faith. Both the growing quality of our individual and corporate lives and the growth of our numbers are crucial to the Faith to Grow program of the 1980s. Concern and attention are being given to the quality of our life together in its growth and the witnessing of God's love to all persons in the numerical expansion of the people of God throughout the world.

To implement the Faith to Grow program a model has been developed to explain the Growth and Expansion process. Involving four dimensions, the model is understood as the "window" through which we see the mission of the church. It is a process, a spiraling cycle, that gives us a visual way of approaching our task.

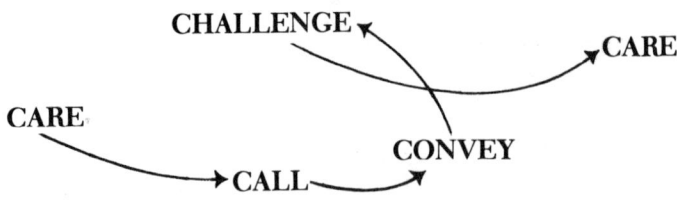

The first step, CARE, is the essence of what has been shared in this chapter. To care is to offer love, healing, reconciliation, nurture, courage, and hope to people. Giving care involves all persons, is a community effort, and reflects care as an all pervasive process. The caring process is the fundamental and primary step toward growth and expansion. As Jesus, responding to the question of which commandment was the greatest, said, "You shall love the Lord your God with all your heart, with all your soul, and with all your mind. This is the great and first commandment. And a second is like it, You shall love your neighbor as yourself" (Matthew 22:37-39, RSV). "There is no other commandment greater than these" (Mark 12:31, RSV).

The task before us all in the 1980s is to take the principles of a caring ministry and make them come alive in the people around us. Our first step is to **CARE**.

Without care the other dimensions of the model lose their power and authority. Without care the model is sterile and lacks warmth and energy. People grow and the community expands when there is first and primarily a climate of care.

The other dimensions of the model—call, convey, and challenge—begin to fall into place once a caring environment is present. A person can begin to hear the CALL of the living Christ when he or she has first experienced a fundamental love and concern. It is because of the experience of care that the call begins to have meaning. The CONVEYING of the message is received once a caring ministry has opened a person to hearing. And the CHALLENGE is accepted once a person feels and understands that he or she is ultimately cared for and loved. The challenge of the gospel of Jesus Christ leads one to a caring ministry, and the cycle is repeated as one grows and expands.

PROGRAMMING FOR PASTORAL CARE IN THE 1980s

The focus for pastoral care is the local congregational unit. It is in the life of the congregation that the experience of God's love is made real and personal. When we are touched by the person sitting next to us, we experience the meaning of pastoral care. It is important that we begin to look for ways of providing this care in our local congregation.

A critical idea in the programming for pastoral care is to emphasize the climate or environment rather than simply the "program." Often we establish a well organized program that ends up taking us away from a climate of care. For example, a "meals on wheels" program that keeps us so busy delivering meals without any personal contact does not give us time to share with each other who we are and what our needs are. To program for pastoral care is to create a climate where we can openly share our pain, hurts, and joys. The crucial part is to establish and emphasize the environment where this can take place. The purpose of the "program" is to provide an arena where we care for each other.

Two biblical images are helpful when establishing a program for pastoral care. The first is the **Shepherd** image. The scriptures are full of accounts where God is viewed as shepherd, giving us a model from which to pattern our caring ministry (Psalms 23, 79, 100; Isaiah 40; Matthew 9:36; 15:24; 18:12-14). A shepherd is one who first of all cares enough to be involved in human need. The care is reflected by the shepherd's willingness to lead and nurture, share and heal, sacrifice and risk. When translating this image into programs for pastoral care the emphasis is on a climate where people can be reconciled and healed.

The second biblical image is **Servant**. The life of Jesus exemplified the model of service, upon which we can base our ministry (Luke 22:27; John 13:4-11; Phil. 2:7-8). A servant is a giver, one who reaches out and empties self in service. A servant is a guider, one who teaches the meaning and application of pastoral care. The servant image can translate into the guiding, nurturing, and sustaining functions of a pastoral care ministry.

Ideas for a shepherding and servant care ministry might include:

1) Small pastoral groups
2) Congregational fellowship activities (for everyone)
   A. Potlucks
   B. Sunday dinner and talent nights
   C. Campfires
   D. Recreation groups
   E. Christmas caroling
   F. Evening media event—slides, films, etc.
3) Congregational weekend retreat
4) Small house churches (e.g. meeting once a month for Sunday worship and study)
5) Small prayer circles
6) Home visiting—by families, couples, priesthood, individuals
7) Skill-building workshops (see the resource section of this chapter)
8) Experiential/learning workshops (see the resource section of this chapter)
9) Lay counseling program (contact Pastoral Care Office, the Auditorium)
10) Meals to the sick, elderly, pregnant, families that have experienced a recent death, etc.
11) Congregational newsletter—sharing personal events, etc.
12) Letter writing—to those in college, service, etc.
13) Priesthood training—interpersonal relationship skills, communication skills, etc.
14) Cradle Roll Program (contact Pastoral Care Office, the Auditorium)

References
1. C. W. Brister, *Pastoral Care in the Church* (New York: Harper and Row), 1964.
2. E. Fromm, *The Art of Loving* (New York: Harper and Row), 1956.

STUDY SUGGESTIONS

1. Discuss the ways in which the brokenness in our lives can come to control us rather than free us to move toward wholeness.
2. Add to and expand the list of ideas for programming pastoral care with the *Shepherd* image.
3. Add to and expand the list of ideas for programming pastoral care with the *Servant* image.
4. Give examples and discuss those examples of how the six principles of pastoral care are important in a ministry of caring and love.
5. Discuss how the implementing principles of pastoral care are important for the church in the 1980s.
6. Find scriptures other than those mentioned in the article that are important to a pastoral care ministry. Discuss these.
7. Compose a responsive reading affirming the worth of persons. It could be read at the close of a study session or used in a worship service.
8. Make a banner that can be placed in your church sanctuary that reflects the meaning(s) of pastoral care for your congregation.
9. Brainstorm and discuss the many different ways pastoral care forms the foundation for Christian

ministry. Relate to the 4 C's in the 1980 Faith to Grow program.
10. Discuss why the author emphasized the "climate" of pastoral care in the programming of pastoral care. What do you think about this? Why? Discuss.

PASTORAL CARE AND THE GROWTH OF PERSONS
by Kay Sheridan

As a counselor I have the extreme good fortune of being involved with people who are struggling to make changes in their lives—in other words, to grow. I often stand in awe and wonder about this growth process. As I wonder I have certain basic questions. What things help or facilitate growth? What things hinder growth? In my church life also I see people struggling to grow, both spiritually and emotionally. I am proud to belong to an institution that is attempting to look at and encourage this personal growth. I believe this is what Pastoral Care is all about—this encouraging of personal growth. In this chapter we will be looking at some of the things that can be done to facilitate growth and some of the things that seem to stand in its way.

WHAT IS GROWTH

Life, at its best is a flowing, changing process in which nothing is fixed. —Carl Rogers

First of all some definition of growth would be appropriate. Just what is it we are wanting to move toward? Sören Kierkegaard has put forth a very simple but all encompassing statement. He calls us "to be that self which one truly is." At first glance this may appear too simplistic; actually it is a very difficult thing to achieve. So much of our time and energy is spent trying to be that which we are not. Almost everything we do is calculated to form an impression. We try to build and maintain the image we want others to see. We do our best to hide behind a shield. "Only you yourself know whether you are cowardly and cruel, or loyal and devout; others do not see you, they make but uncertain conjectures about you; they see not so much your nature as your art."[1] Your art is the mask with which you hide yourself. If you doubt the validity of these statements, look around you at your next party, business meeting, or church function. See how many people are able to be fully who they are at any given moment. "How fragile a thing we see that genuine fellowship to be. For in ordinary life it is impossible always to be laying bare one's heart. One has to enclose it in protective armour."[2] Growth then would be the movement away from facades, expectations, and pleasing others. It would include a movement toward self-direction, acceptance of others, and trust of self. This is not an easy direction, nor is it ever complete. Rather it should be seen as a continuing way of life—always in the process of becoming.

MAKING CONTACT

One has to be a person in order to establish contact with other people.—Paul Tournier

We seem to be caught in a dilemma. Our goal is to grow into the persons we truly are, yet we find ourselves caught within our protective armor, unable to make contact with others in a meaningful way. Few people have had an emphasis in their childhood on learning to make contact with others or even with themselves. Most of us are taught instead how to obey and how to do competent work.

> **Many people look without seeing -**
> **listen without hearing -**
> **speak without meaning -**
> **move without awareness -**
> **touch without feeling.**[3]

It seems two questions need to be answered here. Is this personal contact necessary to our growth? If so, what is necessary for significant contact to take place? In response to the first question, I can say that there are times in my work when I meet with another person and, for whatever reason in myself and in the other, contact is never achieved. We may talk quite pleasantly for the hour, sharing thoughts and experiences, but somehow we manage to avoid being fully present, fully who we are. Contact is not made and rarely does growth happen in these instances. I come away with my pretenses still intact, and so does the client. On the other hand, there are moments when we can touch each other person-to-person rather than pretense-to-pretense; in those moments growth can and does occur.

It would appear that growth comes primarily when we are able to share who we are with another. "We become fully conscious only of what we are able to express to someone else."[4] If I am not able to be who I am it is more difficult for you to be who you are.

I was working with a man who was the husband of a good friend. I wanted very much to be helpful and "do a good job" for her as well as for him. Somehow the sessions were not going well; contact was not being made. I was handling him with kid gloves, allowing my expectations and concern about my inadequacy to separate us. When I recognized this I shared my feelings and doubts with him. In response to my self-disclosure he was able to begin sharing some of his real concerns, and contact was then established. When I became free to allow him to see me as a person with all my imperfections and fears, he was then free to become a person with me—and real sharing could occur. It would seem then that there are two fundamental characteristics of each person. The first is the ability to form relationships; the second is the assuming of responsibility. A true personal relationship, of the sort that makes the person, involves both choice and risk; it lays one open to reply and to the necessity of replying in turn. In other words it becomes a dialogue between two people. When you approach me with honesty, you call forth honesty from me in return, and that allows us both to grow. It would appear then that contact with another person is necessary for growth to occur.

THE RELATIONSHIP

We meet naturally on the basis of our sameness and grow on the basis of our differences.—Virginia Satir

If contact is indeed necessary for growth to occur, what is it that helps this contact to happen? As I look at our concept of growth, I feel I have changed my stance. Previously I have viewed the basic question of pastoral care to be, "How can I treat, help, change, or minister to this person?" Now I see the question to be, "How can I provide a relationship which this person may use for personal growth?" There are many methods we can use which appear very direct and effective. We can lecture, give examples, or actually do things for people, but these have only temporary effect if any. Change appears to come through experience in a relationship. If a certain type of relationship can be provided, people will discover within themselves the capacity to use that relationship for growth and change, and personal development will occur. A very important and comforting factor about pastoral care when viewed this way is that we don't have to make any major changes in people. We don't have to help them grow another head or change their color or age or sex. All the needed parts are there. It is just a case of providing an accepting relationship so persons can get acquainted with the parts they already have.

Several very skilled psychologists have talked about the relationship that they seek to provide in order to facilitate growth. Virginia Satir has summed up her feelings concisely:

Goals for Me

**I want to love you without clutching,
appreciate you without judging,
join you without invading,
invite you without demanding,
leave you without guilt,
criticize you without blaming,
and help you without insulting.
If I can have the same from you
then we can truly meet and
enrich each other.[5]**

Carl Rogers and Milton Mayeroff have also written at length on this topic of the growth-producing relationship. Rogers states, "The degree to which I can create a relationship which facilitates the growth of others as separate persons is a measure of the growth I have achieved in myself."[6] There appear to be several very tangible pastoral care qualities necessary in a relationship before growth can take place. One of the qualities briefly touched on earlier is genuineness. In order to be genuine I need to be myself rather than presenting a facade. Only when I provide the genuine reality which I am can others seek to find their own reality. It is extremely important to be real.

Closely connected to genuineness but with something else to offer is honesty. For a relationship to produce growth I must be able to see the other person and/or the situation as it is, not as I would like it to be or feel it must be. I must also be able to see myself as I am. There must be no gap between what I say and what I feel—how I act and how I think.

Another quality that is key to a growing relationship

is patience. Growth cannot be forced. By being patient I enable others to find their own way in their own time. Patience gives the space to feel and think; it gives room to live. Just as we cannot force a flower to open by pulling the petals apart, we cannot force other people to grow without causing damage. People operate on their own internal time schedules. The most helpful thing we can do is honor them with the assurance that they do have the tools necessary for their own growth. I watched a child enjoying the struggle of learning to tie her own shoelaces. A woman who was also in the room came to her rescue and tied them for her. The shoes were tied "correctly" but the message that was given was "You are inadequate to do this task by yourself." Often we rush in to "fix things" for the other person when the situation actually requires our patient waiting. "The more I am open to the realities in me and in the other person, the less do I find myself wishing to rush in and fix things."[7]

In order to have patience we must also have trust—trust in other people's ability to develop at a pace that is all their own and may in fact be very different from ours. In a relationship that is to produce growth, differences must be at least allowed and hopefully encouraged. "In helping the other grow I do not impose my own direction; rather, I allow the direction of the other's growth to guide what I do, to help determine how I am to respond and what is relevant to such response."[8] In trusting the other I must let go of my expectations and demands. To do so requires an element of risk; it demands a leap into the unknown. In order to take the risks required by trust I also need courage in the relationship. Trust in the other to grow and in my ability to care gives the courage to go into the unknown, but it is also true that without courage such trust would be impossible.

Hope is another needed element to growth. This might be caught up in the concept that not only are we with people as they struggle toward growth, but we are for them as well. We have hope that they will grow, but it is a hope without specific expectations. This kind of hope is not a way of saying that they are not all right as they are. This is not an expression of the insufficiency of the present in comparison with the sufficiency of a hoped for future; rather it is an expression of the plenitude of the present. This is a hope that is alive with a sense of the possible.

Acceptance is also necessary for a relationship to produce growth. "We cannot change, we cannot move away from what we are, until we thoroughly accept what we are. Then change seems to come about almost unnoticed."[9] As long as all our energy is being expended in defending where we are, there is no possibility for change. I was working with a woman who had a drinking problem. All of my skillful reasons about why she should change her behavior brought absolutely no response except denial and further strengthening of her present position. It wasn't until I could hear her and accept her as she was—drinking and all—that change could happen. Acceptance needs to be unconditional, without strings attached, a total prizing of people as beings of worth just as they are. Relationships cannot be built on the premise, *I will accept you if. . . or when*, but rather *You are a person of worth just as you are at this moment.* This total acceptance gives others a sense of safety in which they are free to begin to look at some of their behavior problems. If they don't have to spend their energy defending themselves and their behavior to you, they can use that same energy to move toward becoming the persons they would like to be.

The last quality I shall touch on is understanding. "To care for another person I must be able to understand him and his world as if I were inside it. All actions make sense from his perspective."[10] I believe that all behavior—no matter how destructive and hurtful it may appear—does make sense to the individual. At any given time individuals are acting in the best ways they know how with their background and the immediate situation. If they could do better at the moment they would. All behavior, no matter how negative, is designed to meet certain honorable goals. These goals are:

1. **To survive**
2. **To be in charge of one's self**
3. **To be close to others**
4. **To be creative or productive**
5. **To have a sense of order in one's life**

This may appear to be a very difficult concept at first glance. Let's look at some examples to support it. A family I was working with had a seven-year-old son named David. What brought the family into treatment was the constant fighting between David and his older brother, almost always initiated by David. When we stopped to consider what was going on in this family a very clear pattern emerged. David teased—older brother hit—mother came to David's aid and defense. When the mother began giving more positive attention to David before the fighting began, the misbehavior lessened. It appeared that David's honorable goal was to be close to his mother, but for whatever reasons he was not able to ask for that directly. By creating negative behavior he achieved his purpose.

Joe provides another example of destructive behavior to achieve an honorable goal. He is in danger of losing his job, his wife, and his children because he cannot control his drinking. Yet the only time Joe is free to make decisions for himself, to be in charge of his own life, is when he is drinking. This may not be the case with all alcoholics, but the pattern fits for Joe. Our task is to understand Joe's need for self-direction and assist him in finding more acceptable ways of meeting that goal. This is not to say we need to accept his behavior, but we do need to accept Joe and understand him as he is. If, however, we allow ourselves to be so caught up in the negative behavior that we cannot see Joe's intention or his honorable goal then we cannot fully understand. Joe may not even be aware of the goal behind his negative behavior; however, if we try to look at his world from his vantage point his behavior will make sense and understanding can occur. This type of understanding is the opposite of judging or evaluating.

It seems the key to understanding another is found in being able to accept and understand ourselves. I can understand in you only what I can understand in myself. If I cannot accept and understand my own anger, for example, I will have difficulty with yours.

Carl Rogers sums it up well when he talks about his hopes for a relationship and what the expected outcome will be.

> If I can create a relationship characterized on my part:
> by a genuineness and transparency, in which I am my real feelings;
> by a warm acceptance of and prizing of the other person as a separate individual;
> by a sensitive ability to see his world and himself as he sees them;
> Then the other individual in the relationship:
> will experience and understand aspects of himself which previously he has repressed;
> will find himself more able to function effectively; will become similar to the person he would like to be;
> will be more self directing and self confident;
> will become more of a person, more unique and more self expressive;
> will be more understanding, more acceptant of others;
> will be able to cope with the problems of life more adequately and more comfortably.[11]

THE SYSTEM

Unless we cope with the ways in which modern society oppresses the individual, we shall lose the creative spark that renews both societies and men. Unless we foster versatile, innovative and self-renewing men and women, all the ingenious social arrangements in the world will not help us.[12]

So far we have focused primarily on how people can

relate to each other in a one-to-one relationship in positive, caring, and growth-producing ways. All of us operate within a larger framework also. We are involved in a variety of systems—the family, the work world, the church, and society in general. In our consideration of pastoral care as a facilitator of growth, these other systems also need to be explored.

Just what is a system? Virginia Satir[13] has identified different elements of a system. She feels that any system from as large as a national government to as small as our individual family unit has certain identifiable parts. All systems consist of several individual parts that are essential and related to one another. There are actions and reactions and interactions among the parts that keep changing. Each part acts as a starter to all the other parts.

The parts of a system work like a cake. Cake is made up of several parts—flour, eggs, water, etc.—but when they are put together, the end result is quite different from any of the individual parts separately. Our families and congregations are like that, too. Each is made up of individual people, but the whole is different from any of the parts. Likewise, when there is change within the system—for example growth within one member—all the rest are affected and changed, as is the whole. If twice as much flour is added to the cake, the end result is again different. Therefore each of us has a vested interest in the change that occurs in the others, since we will be directly affected by it.

Any operating system consists of the following parts:
1. A purpose or goal (Why does this system exist?). In the church it might be to bring persons closer to

their God-given potential by bringing them into right relationship with God.
2. The essential parts. In the church this would be the membership—men, women, and children, and designated leaders who come from the membership to fulfill certain tasks and return to it.
3. An order to the parts working. This would include rules within the system and communication among the various parts.
4. Ways of dealing with change from the outside (How does the system deal with the new and different?).

It seems there are two basically different kinds of systems—open and closed. The main difference appears to be in the reaction to change on the part of its members. The open system provides for change and even encourages it. The closed system provides for little or no change. The growth we have been discussing under pastoral care would be seen as change; therefore, it would seem helpful to look at how the different systems would approach growth or change. The closed system evolves from a particular set of beliefs.

1. Persons are basically evil and have to continually be controlled to be good.
2. Relationships have to be closely regulated.
3. There is only one right way.
4. There is always someone who knows what is best for others.

In this system self-worth is secondary to power and performance. Actions are subject to the whims of "the boss." Change is resisted.

The open system has a very different set of beliefs.

1. Self-worth is primary, with power and performance related to it.
2. Actions are the outcome of reality.
3. Change is welcomed and considered normal and desirable.
4. Communication, system, and rules are all related.

As we look at systems and how they relate to pastoral care and growth, it would be helpful to consider four potential troublemakers as identified by Satir.
1. The feelings and ideas one has about oneself—self-worth.
2. The way people work out to make meaning with one another—communication.
3. The rules people use for how they should feel and act—the system.
4. The way people relate to other people and institutions—the link to society.

Acceptance is needed when
1. Self-worth is low.
2. Communication is indirect, vague, and not really honest.
3. Rules are rigid, inhuman, nonnegotiable, and everlasting.
4. The linking to society is fearful, placating, and blaming.

In order for growth to occur we need to establish a system where
1. Self-worth is high.
2. Communication is direct, clear, specific, and honest.

3. Rules are flexible, human, appropriate, and subject to change.
4. The linking to society is open and hopeful.

Let us look a little closer at each of these areas.

SELF-ESTEEM

Feelings of self-worth can only flourish in an atmosphere where individual differences are appreciated, mistakes are tolerated, communication is open, and rules are flexible. — Virginia Satir

There is a great deal of difference between persons whose self-esteem is high and those who have low feelings of self-worth. Integrity, honesty, responsibility, compassion, and love all flow easily from persons who have high self-esteem. They feel that they matter, are important, and have something of value to offer. They are able to ask for help, but also believe they can make their decisions and are their own best resource. Appreciating their worth, they are ready to see and respect the worth of others. They radiate trust and hope.

Other people spend most of their lives with low self-esteem. Because they feel they have little worth, they expect to be cheated, stepped on, and depreciated by others. Expecting the worst, they invite it and usually get it. To defend themselves they hide behind a wall of distrust and sink into loneliness and isolation. Separated from other people they become apathetic and indifferent toward themselves and those around them. If they feel a need to build themselves up, they may be more prone to try to tear others down.

There are certain basic freedoms that need to be established in our systems if we want to encourage feelings of positive self-worth. We need to have
1. **The freedom to see and hear what is here instead of what should be, was or will be.**
2. **The freedom to say what one feels and thinks, instead of what one should.**
3. **The freedom to feel what one feels, instead of what one ought.**
4. **The freedom to ask for what one wants, instead of needing to wait for permission.**
5. **The freedom to take risks in one's own behalf, instead of choosing to be only "secure" and not rock the boat.**[14]

If we could provide these five basic freedoms, people would be more free to be who they really are and feel good about it. Self-esteem would be enhanced. We could then be free to relate to each other in caring and growing relationships.

COMMUNICATION

Communication is the greatest single factor affecting a person's health and his relationship to others.— Virginia Satir

Some words have a great deal of power in our communications. Here are several to use with caution and loving care: I, you, they, it, but, yes, no, always, and should.

I. Many persons avoid using this word because they don't want to bring attention to themselves. When they use "I" they are taking responsibility for their statement. (Example: "I am happy.").

You. This can be used as an accusation, putting the blame on someone else. There is a big difference between "I am feeling angry right now at you," and "You always make me so angry." In the first I assume the responsibility for my statement and feeling. In the second, I am saying that it's your fault I'm angry; I'm blaming you for my feeling.

They. This can be an indirect way of talking about "you." It is also useful in assessing blame. It can even become a combination of negative ideas that are never identified. (Example: "They are the cause of all the trouble.")

It. Like "they," what "it" refers to is often not clear. It may be a hidden "I" message. (Try substituting I for it. Example: "It seems cold" could be changed to "I am cold." This brings person and communication closer together.)

But. This is often used as a way of saying yes and no in the same sentence. *But* tends to negate the first part of the sentence. (Example: "I'd really like to go with you, but I have to study.")

Yes...No. These words are important to clarity. When they are said clearly, and they mean now and not forever, and they relate to an issue rather than a person's value, they are very useful tools of communication. (When your *no* isn't clear, your *yes* may be mistrusted. Also when you are not free to say *no*, *yes* has little meaning.)

Always...never. These words are often used for emotional emphasis rather than being true in the literal sense. "You always make me mad" really means "Right now I am very mad at you." Emotionally laden words tend to harm rather than nurture or enlighten a situation.

Should... ought. These are words that imply there is something wrong with you; in some way you have failed to measure up. "You shouldn't feel that way." Often they are used to indicate a dilemma when a person has more than one direction to go at a time. Their use can be a tip-off that the person is engaged in an internal struggle.[15]

If we can pay attention to our words, to the power that they have and the messages they give, we can move toward clearer communication and more positive contact with others.

THE RULES
No matter what happens, look happy!

Rules are found within all systems. They are an unwritten way of regulating what goes on. Rules have to do with the person's freedom to comment:

What can you say about what you are seeing and hearing?

To whom can you say it?

How do you go about disagreeing or disapproving of someone or something?

How do you question when you don't understand... or can you?

If the rule is that you can talk only about the good, the right, the appropriate, and the relevant, large parts of what actually goes on cannot be commented on. This lack of comment creates distance, pretense, and artificiality. The rules may permit expressing feelings only if they are justified—not because they are there.

"How could you feel like that?" lowers self-esteem by denying the feelings and therefore the person. The rule here would be: "Thou shalt have only justified feelings."

In a family I worked with, the son had been hospitalized with a nervous breakdown. The rule in this family was that others could not talk about the son or his illness, and furthermore, they could not talk about the fact that they couldn't talk about him either.

We need to work at creating systems with rules which support that whatever we are feeling or experiencing is human and therefore acceptable. In this type of system the self can grow. This is not the same as saying all actions are acceptable; however if the feeling is welcome there is a greater chance for growth and more appropriate behavior on the part of the person.

THE LINKING TO SOCIETY

No system, whether it be the family, the church, or any other institution, can exist in a vacuum. All are linked to other systems. These links can be either perceived as positive—opportunities for growth to occur—or threatening—potentially damaging. This positive or negative perception is determined by whether the system is open and therefore accepting of change or closed and struggling against change. If the rules in the system say that "they" (meaning anyone other than "us") are bad, sick, or evil, our response will be a protective one. We will respond out of fear, blame, or an attempt to appease. None of these responses leave much room for positive communication and relationship building. If, on the other hand, we as a system come from a position of strength, appreciating our own worth, and we further perceive the other systems as also having value and something positive to offer, our approach will be more open, positive, and hopeful.

Pastoral care then can facilitate growth on several levels—within the individual, within relationships, within the system, and between systems.

IN CONCLUSION

I have attempted in this chapter to look at pastoral care and the growth of persons. I have defined growth as an attempt to be that self which one truly is. This is accepted as a difficult thing for me to do since I feel I must protect myself behind a mask for fear I might not measure up. Sometimes when I look at you all I see is your mask. In order for us both to grow we need to make contact with each other—person to person. For us to make contact that will encourage growth on both our parts, we need to establish a relationship. Our relationship needs to include such qualities as genuineness, honesty, patience, trust, courage, hope, acceptance, and understanding. We are also operating within a system that may either encourage our growth or repress it. In a system that fosters high self-esteem, clear and direct communication, flexible and appropriate rules, and an open and hopeful linking to society, growth can and does occur.

It seems then that in our growing we are tied to one another. My growth depends on you and the relationships we are able to establish, just as your growth depends on me. Instead of grudgingly acknowledging my dependence on others, I feel gladness in realizing my debt to them and the ties that bind us together. This gratitude remains incomplete until I have expressed my thanks for what I have received. Pastoral care then becomes my way of thanking others for the growth I have been given.

REFERENCES

1. Montaigne, *Essays* (New York: AMS Press), 1892.
2. Paul Tournier, *The Meaning of Persons* (New York: Harper and Row), 1957.
3. Virginia Satir, *Making Contact* (Milbrae, California: Celestial Arts), 1976.
4. *Op. cit.*, Tournier.
5. *Op. cit.*, Satir.
6. Carl Rogers, *On Becoming a Person* (Boston: Houghton Mifflin Co.), 1961.
7. *Ibid.*
8. Milton Mayeroff, *On Caring* (New York: Harper and Row), 1971.
9. *Op. cit.*, Rogers.
10. *Op. cit.*, Rogers.
11. *Op. cit.*, Rogers.
12. John Gardner, *Self Renewal, the Individual and the Innovative Society* (New York: Harper and Row), 1963.
13. Virginia Satir, *Peoplemaking* (Palo Alto, California: Science and Behavior Books, Inc.), 1972.
14. *Op. cit.*, Satir, *Making Contact*.
15. *Op. cit.*, Satir, *Peoplemaking*.

STUDY SUGGESTIONS

1. "To be that self which one truly is." Consider this statement for yourself. In what ways are you spending energy trying to be that which you are not?

In what ways are you spending energy trying to build upon who you are and trying to become who you want to be?
2. Two significant questions are raised in the section on making contact. They are: (1) Is personal contact necessary to our growth? and (2) If so, what is necessary for significant contact to take place? Share together the answers the author gives to these questions. Share together your answers to these questions.
3. The author views the basic question of pastoral care as being "How can I provide a relationship which this person may use for personal growth?" What is your reaction to this question?
4. The author suggests several very tangible pastoral care qualities that are necessary in a relationship before growth can take place. After each quality, write a sentence describing why you feel this quality is necessary in a growing relationship. Share your sentences with each other.

Genuineness:

Honesty:

Patience:

Trust:

Courage:

Hope:

Acceptance:

Understanding:

5. Share together the meaning of a closed and open system. Is your congregation an open or closed system? Discuss this. Is your family an open or closed system? Discuss this with your family.
6. In the section on self-esteem the author describes five basic freedoms that need to be established in systems which encourage feelings of positive self-worth. Are these basic freedoms established in the systems in which you live (e.g., church, family, work)? Share together.
7. Try to identify the rules present in the systems in which you live. Share these rules together. Use the following questions in your discussion:

> What can you say about the things you are seeing and hearing?
> To whom can you say it?
> How do you go about disagreeing or disapproving of something or someone?
> How do you question when you don't understand... or can you question?

THE UNIQUENESS OF PASTORAL CARE
by Joe A. Serig

Pastoral care is the expression of concern by persons toward each other. Among individuals, families, and other primary social groups it is based on the message of the good news of God's love demonstrated in Jesus Christ. This message calls us as disciples into the ministry of reconciliation. The Christian faith affirms that our central need as humans is to actualize the potential with which we are created—to become ourselves, to fulfill the inherent image of God. Such a development cannot be defined in final terms. It is formulated in terms of life relationships—the individual in relationship to God, to other persons, and to self. Christ continually confronts us with this reality.

Pastoral care to individuals, families, and other groups is in reality both the *message* and the *ministry* of God's people. It is not possible to separate relationships from the value of that which they try to communicate. Christian attributes are developed only in relationship with other persons. Such development occurs when one person is associated with another in a relationship of self-giving love. When there is mutual trust and love persons become whole. We most frequently experience the grace of God neither in idealized notions of fancy nor in propositional statements describing intellectual understanding but in the love extended by another person at the point of need. While expressions of God's grace are not limited by the persons seeking to offer ministry, it is in personal terms that grace is most significantly communicated. New creation occurs where the real life needs of persons are confronted by the power of the Holy Spirit. The broken are healed. The prejudiced are enlarged. The bored are stimulated. The lonely find worth. The proud discover purpose and meaning in giving. It is on this level that we experience ourselves as persons before God. Only in the quality of relationship in which caring finds personal expression can the creative and redemptive work of God be manifest.

The gospel is finally communicated in meaningful lived-out relationships. Since every Christian disciple is called to be an agent of God's love pastoral care necessarily involves the growth and development of caring relationships in congregational and community life. It has to do with values, attitudes, and behavior of one person toward another. Pastoral care, therefore, takes seriously the capacity of ordinary persons to bear one another's burdens. The testimony of the Christian community is that as we accept this task we find unique resources of strength both in the power of the Holy Spirit in our midst and in each other.

Specific examples of pastoral care might include visiting the sick, listening to a troubled friend, caring for a family when someone is ill, establishing a counseling center at the church, conducting a weekly program for elderly patients in a nursing home, and providing classes on changing life-styles for singles and/or marrieds. If motivated by a desire to share God's love expressed in Christ, all of these and more can be tangible expressions of pastoral care.

While focusing on this understanding of pastoral care throughout the text, we need to be reminded that pastoral care is only part of the picture of our total life together as a church. This is not to minimize the importance of pastoral care but rather to see its unique relationship to other functional areas of church life. While pastoral care is essential both as a function and in its more tangible program expressions, we need to see this aspect of our equipping ministry in relation to the other church functions—namely

Leadership   **Stewardship**
Worship   **Zionic Relationships**
Christian Education **Missionary Task**

Each of these functional areas should relate to the needs, concerns, problems, and questions with which we deal in our congregational life. Like each part of a finely tuned car, every functional area of congregational life affects the others. Pastoral care should help us keep our primary attention focused on the needs of persons and how the church can relate to those needs as we address all of these program areas.

A brief description of the other six areas of church

program follows. Pastoral care should bring to each of these a focus on the ultimate worth of persons in the sight of God and remind us that the final purpose of our ministry is to bring persons to the testimony of the life and victory of our Lord Jesus Christ.

Leadership

Leadership training and education are always of prime importance in any institution. They are the basis for establishing an effective institutional program. This area carries responsibility for increasing the knowledge base of leaders as well as the experience factor of education and training which is so important. Leaders need to be equipped with an understanding of the needs of persons, with a series of administrative skills, and with the ability to motivate and stimulate people. Pastoral care should bring the perspective to leadership training and development that the worth of persons is central. Thus, leadership development has as a primary focus the giftedness of each person. One of the roles of a leader is to call forth individual gifts and blend them in harmonious ministry. Effective leadership development is fundamental in maximizing the possibility of success in all other program areas.

WORSHIP

Worship includes those activities in which persons acknowledge themselves to be in the presence of God. This includes a wide variety of personal and group activities. The role of worship in the life of the congregation is one of enablement; that is, its final purpose is to call us to fulfill the mission of God in the world through the church. One key to effective worship is that it calls disciples to an acceptance of their missional responsibilities. Worship enriches persons by providing individual and group avenues for experiencing God's Spirit. Whether in the life of a person or the experiences of a congregation, worship is never self-serving. Rather, sound worship invites and stimulates us to involvement with others as God's emissaries. Worship confronts us with an expanding sensitivity to and awareness of

>who we are.
>who we are called to become.
>who God is.
>God's will for us.
>Our mission in the world.

Through hymns, prayers, sermons, films, scripture readings, testimonies, and other means, we are reminded of our commitment to place Christ at the center of our lives and to express God's love in all relationships. In a sense, worship is the starting point for our discipleship. It helps us keep our priorities straight. The sacraments of the church give particular emphasis to linking worship with life needs. This linkage is central to enabling us to be God's agents in the world.

Because worship deals so directly with establishing Christian priorities in our lives, the relationship to pastoral care is rather obvious. The two foundational affirmations of the Christian faith are the ultimate love of God and the worth of persons. Thus worship and pastoral care are intimately related.

CHRISTIAN EDUCATION

In the church a part of the fulfillment and joy of existence depends on our coming to understand and appreciate the principles, complexities, and truths of our lives and of the universe. But of special interest are those understandings vital to our faith, those that are essentially religious perceptions of God's purposes and movement in history and in our lives. These understandings and perceptions help equip and motivate members for mission responsibilities. Thus, the church provides opportunity for open discussion and exploration in the ongoing processes of education. The challenge, excitement, and discovery provided by good Christian education is an attractive feature to both the member and the nonmember. Through Christian education we are called to continually grow in our understanding of our own roles as disciples as well as in our appreciation for the broad Christian heritage and faith which is our foundation.

In relationship to pastoral care, Christian education should equip us with those skills, abilities, and understandings which enable us to move effectively as witnesses and as ministers in the lives of persons with whom we come in contact daily. As illustrated in the introduction to this chapter, pastoral care should call us in our educational endeavors to focus finally on God's concern for people.

STEWARDSHIP

Stewardship is one way of describing the relationship between people and God. All of the resources of life are made available by God the Creator and are to be used to fulfill God's purposes for us. The concept of accountability is applicable both to individuals and groups. A basic part of accountability is evaluation of the extent to which personal and group goals are being met. Responsible stewardship requires a commitment to establishing objectives, identifying available resources, determining strategies and programs, implementing a course of action, and evaluating results.

Stewardship is a call to quality living. It involves setting priorities of time, talent, treasure, and energy, so that the mission of the church might be expressed in real life situations. On the congregational level this suggests that all expenditures of time, energy, and dollars will be continually evaluated in light of the demands of the gospel and the needs of persons. Thus, the relationship of stewardship to pastoral care is central. This relationship deals heavily with the underlying value structure of our decisions (i.e. the reasons for our behavior).

ZIONIC RELATIONSHIPS

It is in Zionic relationships that the church's commitment to changing the structures of society which affect the lives of people is most visibly demonstrated. The ultimate Christian values of the worth of persons and the supreme love of God call us to address social concerns as well as individual needs. In Zionic relationships the church expresses the realization that we do not live in isolation but in community. Group relationships and institutions which are destructive of persons need transformation and redemption. Therefore, the congregation becomes involved with the political, economic, and social forces which shape and mold the lives of persons. Schools, governmental bodies, businesses, and recreational institutions become areas of Christian concern and action. We enter into these activities so "the kingdoms of this world may be constrained to acknowledge that the kingdom of Zion is in very deed the kingdom of our God and his Christ" (Doctrine and Covenants 102:9b).

Pastoral care should inform our Zionic relationships—that is, the church is reminded in all of its attempts to establish quality community relationships that the central focus must be the worth of persons and the need for gospel-centered values to be demonstrated in all community relationships. Pastoral care also reminds us that in these relationships we are not attempting to shape people to our image of what they should be but rather to open their lives to receive the call from God that they are loved and accepted as persons of worth.

MISSIONARY TASK

Involvement in the missionary task of the church is essentially a call to share the good news of God's love in Christ. It is the church's commitment to people where they are. It calls for contact with people in their present situations for the purposes of personal redemption and renewal. Being a missionary involves much more than telling people about the church, although that is an important aspect of our task. Our larger concern for persons calls us to share with them their joy, suffering, and anxiety. This mutual giving and receiving, which are natural expressions of our own discipleship, will assist others in opening their lives to the new possibilities which God's power will motivate within them. In this sense the missionary task of the church is pastoral care turned outward—that is, to those not members of our fellowship.

This sharing of the good news is the lifeblood of the church. The congregational functions of pastoral care, education, worship, and stewardship are enabling and equipping ministries to help us answer God's call to participate in the world in bringing redemptive ministry. In addressing the missionary task we are to focus primarily on one-to-one relationships, although in reality we often find it difficult to make a distinction between the missionary task and Zionic community relationships. The reason is that the needs of persons and the problems of communities are so intricately related.

CONCLUSION

Although the functions of congregational life have been described separately, it is important to realize that they are not entirely separable. It is not possible to say that a particular activity or program of the church involves just one function and not the others. For example, is it not true that within the context of the Sunday morning worship service the functions of education, pastoral care, the missionary task, and stewardship may all be present? Is worship entirely absent from the church school program? The overlapping and interrelatedness are inevitable... and potentially helpful. The work of the church, God's work, is whole and integrated rather than a hodgepodge of unrelated activities and functions. It is important to recognize that we can identify separate functions for organizational and planning purposes, but at the same time embrace the "oneness" of the work in which we are called. Pastoral care should help us in this process by continually reminding us that it is ultimately God's concern for the worth of persons that must be the focus of our ministry.

The purpose of the church is to be an agent of God's love so that redeeming love is expressed with conviction and power in the lives of individuals and societies. This may or may not result in persons seeking membership in the Reorganized Church of Jesus Christ of Latter Day Saints. When it does, let us rejoice in that blessing to the church. When it does not, let us continue to share with them the foundations of our faith in loving terms so that their lives might continue to be enriched by the blessing of God's Spirit. The church invites those separated from God, from themselves, and from each other to be made one by the power of love. Just as Christ did not violate the worth of persons but sought to help people fulfill their potential, so the church is called to enable persons to establish and maintain relationships which uplift, sustain, and ultimately redeem. This is the central focus not only of pastoral care but of all ministries of the church.

Since the needs of persons (and the world) provide the agenda for church program, the quality of our life together is significant in relation to our mission as a church. In our relationships together we attempt within the church to faithfully respond to God's call by sharing the love and peace which centers in Christ. The gospel intersects our situations in life with the testimony of Jesus Christ so that we become empowered as "new persons in Christ." It is, after all, persons to whom we seek to minister and bring to an awareness of the testimony of Christ in their lives.

A healthy congregation will consider all of the functions suggested earlier in this chapter as vital. In our car, if one of the cylinders is not functioning properly there is a loss of power and we may fail to reach our destination. In our church we need to keep all cylinders of our congregational program working in harmonious relationship. The particular "power" provided by the pastoral care function is that it reminds us that all we do must finally be seen as ministering significantly in the lives of people as our efforts are enhanced by God's presence through the power of the Holy Spirit. While pastoral care is the focus of this text it needs to be seen in relationship to the total life of the church. The call of our Lord to go into the world and bear witness of him is the central focus of our life together as well as our outreach ministries.

STUDY SUGGESTIONS

1. The author presents the following definition of pastoral care. It
   1) is the expression of concern by persons toward each other.
   2) is based upon the message of the good news of God's love demonstrated in Jesus Christ.
   3) is in reality both the message and the ministry of God's people.

    4) involves the growth and development of caring relationships in congregational and community life.

Discuss the meaning of each statement along with the individual and congregational implications.

2. The author states, "We most frequently experience the grace of God neither in idealized notions of fancy nor in propositional statements describing intellectual understanding, but in the love extended by another person at the point of need." What is your reaction to this statement? Has this been your experience?
3. After presenting specific examples of pastoral care, the author states, "If motivated by a desire to share God's love expressed in Christ, all of these and more can be tangible expressions of pastoral care." How does this statement further explain pastoral care?
4. The other functional areas of church life (leadership, worship, Christian education, stewardship, Zionic relationships, and missionary task) are defined along with a statement concerning how pastoral care affects each one. Discuss each function and its relation to pastoral care. How are these functions lived out in your congregational life? Does pastoral care affect every other function in your congregation? In what ways can your congregation improve its functioning?
5. The functions are not entirely separable. They are interrelated and overlap each other. The author says, "This is inevitable and potentially helpful." Why might this be so? Do you agree?

PASTORAL CARE: MEETING HUMAN NEEDS
by S. Lee Pfohl

INTRODUCTION

One Sunday morning I arrived at a church some distance from my home. As I entered the room where the adult Christian education class was in progress, several people looked at me and smiled warmly. My reaction was, "They are really pleased to see me." I was surprised at the intensity of my good feelings in being welcomed and accepted.

At the time this occurred I was a district president in Ontario, Canada, and was visiting one of the branches in the district. I liked the people and what I was doing. It gave me an opportunity to serve God in the work to which I have committed my life. My days were filled with ministering to people, attending meetings, planning, administrative detail, scripture study, and class and sermon preparation. I felt needed and useful. As I reflected on the strong feelings generated when welcomed by caring friends, I became aware that something had been missing in my life. While I had been pastorally caring for others I had not been conscious of receiving pastoral care from the members of the church who wished to nurture me.

MEETING HUMAN NEEDS THROUGH PASTORAL CARE

Human needs calling for pastoral care are extensive and are met by both crisis and preventive care. Crises burst into our lives; some with little or no warning. Accidents occur suddenly and are a crisis originally for the injured and next for family and friends, depending first on the magnitude of the accident, next upon the number and the severity of the injuries. Those who care must sort out the situation to determine who they can help, what they need, and how they can help. Efforts at pastoral care may focus first on the family and next on the victims, depending on the circumstances.

Crises in addition to accidents include serious illness, death, divorce, family conflict, separation, job loss, and financial problems. We try to find some way to express pastoral care when we are confronted with a crisis. How helpful we are depends on our relationship with those in need, our having adequate information, how extensive our practical knowledge and skill in helping are, and how willing we are to aid in the immediate crisis until it is under control.

My need on the Sunday morning previously mentioned was not a crisis, yet the caring revealed was important to my life. The experience reminded me of several things. While serving others is important in my life, receiving and being served is necessary as well. We share a common humanity as creatures who exist through the power and grace of our Creator. We are never really self-sufficient. We are blessed to have each other. The smiles which greeted me warmed my heart and met my need for love and acceptance through pastoral care.

Preventive care can keep some human needs from escalating into crises. We often see signs of serious marriage and family problems before they reach a critical stage. We can be alert to changes in relationships which reflect more intense human needs. A young mother limited by several preschool children at home may need someone to assist her both by baby-sitting occasionally and by helping her sort out her needs and opportunities.

Visible friction between a middle-age couple, whose children have recently moved from home, reveals a need to deal with the changing relationships which occur when two who became three or more are again two. Preventive care ministers to the need before it becomes a crisis.

A major change in the attitudes of a teen-ager may be signs of growing up or of a potential crisis. In providing preventive pastoral care we reach out to support and to learn which of the two is happening. We don't stop there, however, for affirmation of the growing person and love and friendship offered to those in trouble are all expressions of pastoral care in response to human need.

Human needs are physical, mental, emotional, spiritual.... Pastorally caring people respond appropriately because they are concerned and because they discern human need. The process of becoming an effectively caring people is not automatic. It begins as a response to the love of God which penetrates our lives. We are called to be human agents of that love so that we may convey it and challenge others to share in the task.

LIMITING VIEWS OF PASTORAL CARE

Although we may see many human needs in the lives of those around us we may hold a number of limiting views of pastoral care. One is that pastoral care is something provided only by church leaders. Second, pastoral care applies only to crises. Third, human needs are simply problems to be solved. Fourth, pastoral care is something provided by the strong for the weak. Fifth, pastoral care is limited to formal situations at church or by appointment in the home. Each of these limiting views hinders the ministry of pastoral care.

We frequently refer to the presiding elder as our pastor and expect him to care. As one who hopes to have a pastor's heart (and one who has been a pastor) I often have been overwhelmed by the abundant human needs in the lives of those around me and have looked for help to respond to those needs. If we have a limiting view of pastoral care we may expect the pastor and the other local church leaders, both the ordained and the unordained, to carry the full responsibility. If not we may feel shut out or wonder why they aren't more effective. When this happens everyone loses, beginning with the people whose needs are unmet and extending to others whose unused gifts go to waste and to leaders who become overburdened and burned out.

The very nature of the body of the church is that the body strengthens people and people strengthen the body. We have the need to receive and to give. I am convinced that pastoral care is a calling for all those associated with the church, including members, children, and friends. Each of us at different times in our lives can see and respond to a variety of the human needs of others. Our individual uniquenesses and our variety of life experiences prepare us to be living expressions of pastoral care in meeting the needs of many people.

Children can meet human needs through pastoral care. Last summer I was meeting with families at a workshop on Family Clusters. At one of our sessions five families celebrated in an activity involving worship, songs, games, and testimony. We created a circus in which each child selected an adult partner in the center ring. Brenda, a ten-year-old girl, chose me. She proceeded to make herself up as a bear and me as a monkey. We put on an act in turn and joined the big parade. Being chosen by a child met some of my needs; being helped to relax and play like a child met others. I felt valued and happy through the caring of this little girl.

Youth seem to have a particular affinity for the aged. Many needs on both sides are met when pastoral care brings them together. Young people's sharing an openness and vitality toward life is refreshing and invigorating to the aged. And older adults often share a wisdom and firm foundation needed by the young. When they pastorally care for each other, both are enriched.

Seeing pastoral care as exclusive to meeting crises is a limiting view. In the extreme, seeing the need in a crisis and meeting it successfully can be a matter of immediate survival for a life, a marriage, or a family. Crises are easily identified and, although more stressful for the helper, they can also be more rewarding if the crises are resolved. People in crisis need help and should not be avoided. But if we wait for crises to develop before helping occurs, it may be too late to save a marriage or stabilize a family. Firefighters do not simply wait to fight fires; they try to prevent them. Similarly, a caring climate needs to be created so preventive care can minister to people's needs.

Another limiting view of pastoral care is seeing human needs as problems to be solved rather than people crying out to be helped in the midst of life. The focus instead of the person becomes the problem. This occurs when we attach labels and begin to concentrate on specific problems such as divorce, illness, communication breakdown, drugs, or loneliness instead of focusing on the needs of the people involved. We depersonalize others when we treat them as problems needing attention rather than as persons who need care, support, and companionship. People who fall into a problem-solving syndrome become impersonal in behavior. I am reluctant to call what they do "pastoral care."

Seeing pastoral care simply as the strong helping the weak is a limiting view. Sometimes our strength and knowledge are necessary to provide pastoral care, but to see this as the exclusive model for pastoral care can ultimately result in greater harm than good. All of us need opportunity to give what we can. Gratitude changes to anger and hate when we are held in controlled dependency by others. My wife has reminded me that I need to accept what others want to do for me so that they can express their caring and use their gifts. It has been said in a number of ways that the best gift can be helping others to help themselves.

A limiting view of pastoral care is that it occurs only in formal meetings at church, by appointment at home, or in a hospital setting. While it does occur in these and other settings, the limiting factor is to see it only in a formal, structured situation. Telephone calls, chance encounters, social or sports events, and picnics also can present occasions for pastoral care. Human needs surface under a variety of circumstances, and in a pastoral care environment there are people available to see and to help.

Another limited view of pastoral care is seeing human needs as negative, or helping only unhappy people. Many people need to be able to celebrate a variety of basically happy experiences or achievements. It is obvious that the birth of a child is potentially a joyous event. This joy is multiplied when shared with a caring family and friends. A career promotion seems brighter when we can tell others who care for us and can share our happiness. Musicians expand their talent when they have an audience. Sharing happiness can become a major part of pastoral care.

AN EXPANDING VIEW OF PASTORAL CARE

Although pastoral care may be defined as a function, it is lived out most abundantly as a life-style. I am blessed with a mother-in-law who is a pastorally caring person. For many years she taught nursery class in church school. The children in her class responded to her love by telling her, with great excitement, about the important events in their lives. They felt her love and opened themselves to her. Probably a number of those children, now grown, feel good about coming to church because their early experiences were so meaningful.

Some of the factors which influence a caring life-style are love, values, and attitudes. The importance of love in the gospel is beautifully stated in the New Testament, Chapter 13 of I Corinthians:

> If I speak with the eloquence of men and of angels, but have no love, I become no more than blaring brass or crashing cymbal. If I have the gift of foretelling the future and hold in my mind not only all human knowledge but the very secrets of God, and if I also have that absolute faith which can move mountains, but have no love, I amount to nothing at all. If I dispose of all that I possess, yes, even if I give my own body to be burned, but have no love, I achieve precisely nothing.
>
> This love of which I speak is slow to lose patience—it looks for a way of being constructive. It is not possessive: it is neither anxious to impress nor does it cherish inflated ideas of its own importance.
>
> Love has good manners and does not pursue selfish advantage. It is not touchy. It does not keep account of evil or gloat over the wickedness of other people. On the contrary, it is glad with all good men when truth prevails.
>
> Love knows no limit to its endurance, no end to its trust, no fading of its hope; it can outlast anything. It is, in fact, the one thing that still stands when all else has fallen.

> For if there are prophecies they will be fulfilled and done with, if there are "tongues" the need for them will disappear, if there is knowledge it will be swallowed up in truth. For our knowledge is always incomplete and our prophecy is always incomplete, and when the complete comes, that is the end of the incomplete.
> When I was a little child I talked and felt and thought like a little child. Now that I am a man my childish speech and feeling and thought have no further significance for me.
> At present we are men looking at puzzling reflections in a mirror. The time will come when we shall see reality whole and face to face! At present all I know is a little fraction of the truth, but the time will come when I shall know it as fully as God now knows me!
> In this life we have three great lasting qualities—faith, hope and love. But the greatest of them is love.
> Follow, then, the way of love, while you set your heart on the gifts of the Spirit.
> —J. B. Phillips, *The New Testament in Modern English.*

A life-style which demonstrates continual attempts to reach such an ideal of love will be one which demonstrates pastoral care.

Our internalized values help to shape our life-style. An important value found in the gospel involves the worth of persons. "How much are you worth?" The question does not indicate whether I am asking your net financial worth, the current price of the chemical contents of your body, what value your knowledge, skills, gifts, and talents have to our culture, or how much another person may value you. If the question is to include all of these factors, then the answer would indicate that each of us has a unique worth. In the Christian faith the measure of the worth of persons is revealed in the atonement. One scripture which expresses this is, "Yet the proof of God's amazing love is this; that it was while we were sinners that Christ died for us" (Romans 5:7, J. B. Phillips, The New Testament in Modern English). Pastoral Care is based on the worth of all persons.

There are other values which influence our efforts to provide pastoral care in response to human needs. A few years ago I took a course on pastoral values at the Menninger Foundation. There we examined our values toward aging, criminal injustice, death, single lifestyles, and self-identity. (There are many more—values toward women, children, illness, nations, races, sexuality. etc.) Although we may have firm values on many of these issues, we may not have resolved all of them. A severe illness or the death of someone we love will often find us reexamining our values concerning death.

Our attitudes often reveal our values. If we dislike or fear growing old we reflect this in our attitudes; it is most clearly seen by older people and limits our capacity to minister to them. Our values toward the opposite sex, children, other races and cultures are usually very visible.

An enlarged perception of pastoral care needs includes many things. Some needs are more general. We all need to give and to receive. Children grow to resent their parents if they are kept in the helpless position of always receiving and never being valued for what they can give. Many a wise parent has suffered through the difficulty of having children wanting to help and taking more time and making more work than if the parent had completed the task alone. The time we spend and the quality of it speaks volumes to our children about their worth to us. Clarifying our values is an important step in the process of developing our capacity to help others.

Lives are enriched when people engage in pastoral care. One year at a senior high camp we were able to invite a dozen youth, who had been hospitalized for mental and emotional problems, to spend an afternoon at camp. They were ready to be released from the hospital but needed a good experience to help prepare them. The youth at the camp were anxious about extending the invitation. Before they invited the patients we talked the matter through and arranged both a program of activities and a pattern for relating. Several things occurred. Careful observation indicated that everyone had a good time. The youth from the camp discovered that they could be themselves and just be friends. Those from the hospital not only shared fully but seemed to draw out some of the quieter campers. When the visitors returned to the hospital we processed the experience and found that the campers were overwhelmingly enthusiastic. They not only learned some things about themselves but appreciated the worth of others more. Two days later the campers visited their new friends at the hospital by their invitation and the support of the hospital administration. Several campers remarked that they felt they had received more than they gave. Others said that they had learned that the hospitalized people were not strange at all—just people. The campers didn't judge; instead they were accepting.

RELATIONSHIPS AND CARING

Central to being with people in moments of happiness, stress, achievement, loss, grief, illness, and recovery is the relationship which exists and develops. Something happens to us when we trust ourselves to others and express our deeper feelings. These times are not easily forgotten. Life takes on shades and tones of meaning. Future meetings with people with whom we have shared meaningful moments are filled with both memories and expectations. Strangers become friends who understand something of what we know and who we are. Most of us know people who are special to us because our lives have intertwined and our minds and hearts have touched.

A caring friend helps us to see things as they really are rather than as we may have created them in our own mind. A story we use in our family illustrates this.

A man driving his car in a rural area at night had a flat tire. Unfortunately he discovered he didn't have his tire jack in the car. In the distance he saw a farmhouse light and started walking. As he did so he went through the following thinking process. "I'll ask the farmer if I may borrow a jack so I can change the tire. Since I'm a stranger he might think I won't return it. Well, I can give him a deposit." As he walked the light still seemed a long way off and he began to worry. "The farmer might ask me to leave a deposit and pay to use the jack. Well, I guess five dollars would be okay. But maybe he might want twenty dollars or more." In the distant farmhouse he saw the lights go out, and he became even more disturbed. "Now I'm going to have to get the farmer out of bed and he probably will be angry." The motorist became more and more agitated as he approached the house. When he finally arrived at the door he began knocking loudly. After a time the farmer answered and the incensed motorist, shouted, "You can keep your old jack!"

It takes a reasonably close relationship before one person can talk with another about experiences in which either may have a one-sided or distorted view. It is possible for us to accept differing views from those with whom we are free to exchange information and test our perceptions.

A very important factor in relationships is trust. Several years ago at a church reunion we were engaged in a very competitive baseball game. In the last half of the ninth inning with a player on second, the batter hit a fly ball along the right field line. The runner on second crossed third and made it home. The catcher was almost sure it was a foul ball. The umpire's vision had been blocked. The catcher turned to the first base coach of the opposing team and said, "Leroy, we can trust you; was the ball fair or foul?" Leroy responded, "The ball was foul." Everyone accepted it because they trusted Leroy. They had established a relationship and he demonstrated an integrity which permitted them to trust him.

Caring relationships require dependable and appropriate behavior if they are to last and grow. Caring needs to be consistent. We can't establish much of a friendship with someone who greets us warmly one day and is cool and indifferent another. Some elements which are necessary in sharing pastoral care are caring, seeing, hearing, and communicating. We actively relate to others because we care; this influences the entire relationship. We see a lot more than the surface of those we care for. Often with a glance we can discern that a friend is worried, sad, excited, or happy. Hearing what is said both in content and tone is essential. Sharing what is happening occurs through all kinds of direct and subtle communication. In the interactions of life with friends we test our observations, enlarge our understandings, give ourselves, and enrich our lives. Such interchange occurs when people learn they can count on us. We find ourselves becoming dependable, consistent, caring disciples when we value others and apply ourselves to becoming friends.

PASTORAL CARE AND SELF-UNDERSTANDING

This seems an appropriate time to take a look at ourselves—individually and collectively. Each of us is uniquely an individual identified by our appearance, family, community, nation, age, career, church, friends, etc. Some of our life elements change very little; others are dynamic. If we are to serve pastoral care needs, we need to have a realistic understanding of ourselves as we are now and some idea of what we may become. In our self-inventory we need to ask, "What kind of person am I? What does my knowledge, skill, talent, and personality consist of? What are my strengths? What is possible for me to accomplish in serving others on a short- and long-term basis?" While answering these questions we need to remember that there is no one who can really replace us in life; we are unique.

Although we must accept responsibility and act for ourselves, there are many things a group can do that are impossible for one of us alone. Just recognizing ourselves as members of a congregation makes the body of the church available to us. We can open up to receive pastoral care and join in the task of serving the needs of others both in and out of the church. Caring and sharing act as leaven in us and the church.

It is valuable for us as members of a congregation and/or subgroups to take a collective look at who we are and what we *can* do, as well as what we *are* doing. I have been very impressed with the expansion of knowledge and talent among church members in the last decade. Efforts to collect information and total talents by congregations are very revealing.

We need to gain a balanced view of ourselves, including our numerical size, financial strength, extent of active participation, leadership potential, and much more. We need to reaffirm our faith, our commitment, and our calling. We are in a better position to respond congregationally to pastoral care needs when we have adequate self-understanding.

PROVIDING PASTORAL CARE

We need to give attention to meeting the primary human needs of food, clothing, and shelter. Although these needs are not as great in the Western world, where there are government programs and agencies, there are still people around us who have these needs. The church's monthly oblation offering is used to help meet them. It provides temporary aid in emergencies which are not met by existing agencies. Including the oblation offering as a regular part of the monthly Communion service emphasizes the church's symbolic and functional commitment to meeting human needs. This demonstrates through worship that the church not only cares but also gathers funds each month to provide needed help.

In Third World countries the human need for food is so urgent that it often overshadows the need for clothing and shelter. As a church we lack the capacity to meet even a small portion of these necessities. We do, however, need to do what we can wherever we can plant the church. In those places pastoral care begins with finding ways to help the poor meet their own primary needs for food, clothing, and shelter.

In the Western world we are able, through pastoral care, to provide for a wide range of human needs, including primary ones. We must remember that all of us are called to meet human needs through pastoral care. We must develop preventive ministry. We must see people, not problems, as central to what we are doing. We must recognize that all people have their strengths and weaknesses, and that pastoral care means sharing our strengths and weaknesses with each other in an equal and caring environment. We must see pastoral care occurring wherever and whenever human needs appear. And last, we must see pastoral care as people sharing in a full range of life experiences, including crisis, loss, gain, grief, and happiness.

Although there are many practical ways we can learn to meet human needs through pastoral care, it is not simply a method. Pastoral care is a way of life. As we begin to perceive our role in the church as including responsibility for pastoral care we will recognize that it embraces a life-style, for it searches out ways to express love appropriately in response to human needs. We are called to expand our views of pastoral care and to actively develop a life-style in which we share our Christian love with others.

Pastoral care begins when people recognize the human needs of others and respond in love to meet those needs as best they can. Person-to-person ministry is central to continuing pastoral care; however the pastoral unit or congregation makes possible the delivery and development of pastoral care to a greater degree than the same number of people isolated from each other. An advantage is that in a congregation we give strength to each other, thus providing a supportive environment for pastoral care. Together we can share information about people and their needs and choose who can best respond. Our accumulated knowledge of who needs care and what can be done is greater. We can begin to organize our efforts to become effective as a body of people who live a pastoral care life-style. We can harmonize and humanize our caring.

In succeeding chapters the means and methods of congregational pastoral care will be explored more fully. Human needs are so great that they cry for our response.

STUDY SUGGESTIONS

1. What is meant by preventive care? How is it different from crisis care? How are you involved in pre-

ventive care? How is your congregation involved in preventive care?
2. The author discusses the following limiting views of pastoral care:
   a. Pastoral care is something provided only by church leaders.
   b. Pastoral care applies only to crises.
   c. Human needs are simply problems to be solved.
   d. Pastoral care is something done by the strong for the weak.
   e. Pastoral care is limited to formal situations at church or appointments in the home.
   f. Pastoral care deals only with negative needs and unhappy people. What is your reaction to these limitations? Are you aware of other limitations? Which limitations are present in your congregation? district? stake? What can be done to eliminate the limitations so that a broader pastoral care ministry can exist?
3. The author shares an expanded view of pastoral care by defining it as a life-style which individuals and congregations develop. This caring life-style enriches the helper as well as those being helped. What is your reaction to defining pastoral care in this way?
4. In the section on "Relationships and Caring" the author discusses some positive results of caring relationships. After reviewing what the author has said, add other positive results that you have experienced from caring relationships.
5. The author suggests that people are in a better position to respond individually and congregationally to pastoral care needs when they have

adequate self-understanding. It may be helpful for you to make a self-inventory for yourself and your congregation. Fill out the following from both perspectives:

What kind of person (congregation) are you?

What does your knowledge, skill, talent, and personality consist of?

What are your strengths?

Possible accomplishments on a short-term basis?

Long term?

6. The author's view of a healthy approach to pastoral care includes:
   a. Providing for a wide range of human needs, including the primary needs.
   b. Believing all are called to meet human needs.
   c. Developing a crisis and preventive ministry.
   d. Seeing people, not problems, as central.
   e. Recognizing strengths and weaknesses of each person, and providing ministry in an equal and caring environment.
   f. Seeing pastoral care occurring whenever and

wherever human needs appear.
g. Seeing pastoral care as people sharing in a full range of life experiences, including crisis, loss, gain, grief, and happiness.

What is your reaction to this view of pastoral care?

CARING IN THE FAMILY
by Irene Jones

Grandma was a large woman. Her ample proportions seemed barely adequate to accomodate her abundant soul. Life was rough for her and her large family. They were poor in a time when life was pretty hard even for folks who were not poor. To appreciate Grandma you must know a little about Grandpa. He was an unusual man. He had a lot of very flexible idiosyncracies. In fact, he seemed to receive direction for his life from a source that defied logic and was not subject to compromise but subject to frequent change by his own initiation. He was a great gentleman and a complex person, a person with whom life could be quite complex. So Grandma had Grandpa, a daughter, eight sons, and all the grandchildren. In my memory it was Grandma's family. It seemed that she could and did care for her family with her whole life.

Gentility and genuineness were the hallmarks of Grandma. I thought she was a grand lady. She would corset herself, do her hair on top of her head with imitation tortoise shell combs, wear her best clothes, and go out to face the world confidently. When at home she loved to go barefoot and dress comfortably. At all times, when she appeared in church as a grand lady or barefoot under the clothesline, Grandma's face was lit with a touch of mirth. Lines of merriment played around her eyes and mouth. Oh, how I remember her laughter! Her whole body laughed and when she cried her whole body cried... and sometimes tears and laughter were intermixed.

Grandma was a compassionate woman, but she was not indulgent. We had to meet her standards of behavior. She treated us with respect, and we had great respect for her. She was honest and open and accepting. She knew how to love us and make us feel important, but there was nothing saccharine about her love. She was sturdy, and we should be sturdy.

Grandma's love focused in most sharply on her large family. Love was to be lived out, not demonstrated by hugs and kisses. We experienced her love as she sang and played and told stories. In the kitchen she prepared hot biscuits and baked beans as expressions of love. The little visits we had after a meal were special. Grandma thought it was good to leave the table and sit awhile before getting back into the kitchen with dirty dishes. In those short times of laughter and "letting the food settle" we came to understand what was important to Grandma. Her values made a great impact on my young life.

Grandma died when I was sixteen. I remember trying to comfort my mother at that time, who said, "Oh, I don't grieve for her, but what will we do without her?

There will be such a vacancy in our lives!" Of course there was, but life went on, and we carried on without Grandma—but not really, because her presence lived on and still does. I think my ideas about family life have their deepest roots in my ideas about Grandma's family—a family stable and loyal, open and honest, flexible and adaptable. Grandma's reverence for life and appreciation for the common things that occur daily have deeply influenced me. I believe that my feelings about pastoral care in the family are inseparably related to "growing up" in Grandma's family.

Traditionally families are expected to provide food, clothing, and shelter for their members. In families where there is not sufficient income, that can be a difficult task. In other families where financial resources are more than adequate it may be fairly easy to see that the basic needs are met. But persons need and must have more than food, clothing, and shelter, as important and necessary as these things are. Everyone needs to be loved. The unique way in which love may be expressed in the family can be described as pastoral care. The term itself suggests a kind of everyday, earthy concern and perhaps refers to Jesus as the shepherd who loved his own and gave himself for the defense and the freedom and the life of his sheep. He offered them food and pasture that nourished them unto eternal life. He provided for his care to continue by means of the Holy Spirit, which would tend, feed, shepherd, lead, and unite the flock when he was no longer present. The New Testament metaphor of Jesus as the shepherd and his people as the sheep makes clear that Jesus was not a hireling. Perhaps this is not to suggest that good care givers cannot be hired. Other scripture references help us to know that the servant is worthy of hire, but the scriptures do emphasize the importance of eagerness and willingness to serve in pastoral roles. So in the family lacking worldly goods and in the family having an abundance of worldly goods, the task of pastoral care is the same. Persons in the family must receive and experience love.

Just as many of my ideas about family life came out of Grandma's family, most of us get our ideas about how a family functions from the family of our origin. While the immediate family is of signal importance, the larger extended family including grandparents, uncles, aunts, and cousins plays a significant part in the way we image our own family. Many come from a line of nurturing families; many others come from a line of less nurturing, less loving, less caring families. In either case change is possible and can occur. In some cases families will make changes to improve the quality of life, and in other cases change may occur that produces poorer quality of life. Persons who are committed to improving the quality of life in their families will seek to increase and improve both the quantity and quality of care given to family members.

The makeup of families varies. Today there are many single-parent families in which the children and one parent are together most of the time, and the children spend short periods with the other parent. Families may be composed of grandparents and grandchildren. The grandchildren may be cousins from different families. Blended families in which there are stepchildren and stepparents are becoming more numerous. Grown brothers and sisters may live together as a family. Large and small groups of persons, unrelated by blood ties, may establish a home, sometimes called a commune, and live as a family. A variety of intimate groups may comprise a family and carry out the pastoral care function.

Not only does the composition of families differ but the systems by which similar families operate may be very different. There are many functional family systems, and each family operates out of its own system. Healthy, caring, productive persons may live in a variety of different family systems. Adequate pastoral care may take place in these families that differ widely from each other.

I have tried to identify the qualities of pastoral care that we incorporated into our family life. I think we have provided warmth, light, security, and sanctuary. All members of the family have shared these qualities. Even when the children were very young they contributed to the caring atmosphere and activity of our home.

THE FAMILY PROVIDES WARMTH

Can you recall the feeling of being chilled? Perhaps when you were very young you were not dressed warmly and you had to walk home from school on a winter afternoon when the chill index was surely too low to record. Remember the tender feelings that surged through your whole being when family members met you at the door and started ministering to your needs for warmth? As your cold shoes were removed and you were wrapped in warm blankets the stiffness and hurting began to lessen. Warm soup helped to quiet your chattering teeth. The care of your parents and brothers and sisters almost caused the tears to flow. I can recall such an experience—and many similar ones—when I felt deeply cared for by my family. I believe that our children have experienced this caring where physical needs have been met with warmth.

Warmth is more than physical comfort. Warmth in the family means feeling embraced by family members. It's a kind of pervasive climate in which family members feel accepted and understood. Warmth in the family gives members a sense of well-being, a strength to say "yes" to life. You have probably discovered many ways to radiate warmth in your family life. I will share some of the ways we have learned to bring warmth into our family.

All conversations in the family are personal and confidential. I will always remember the hurt in Rusty's eyes when I very innocently but ignorantly quoted to a friend something he had said to me in conversation. He was very young and what he had said was no secret, but I had betrayed his confidence. My sorrow was deep, and Rusty's hurt was deep; repentance and forgiveness were a part of that experience. I wish I could say that I never made that mistake again. I did. At least from that time there has always been a consciousness that conversations are precious and confidential. When members of the family share with each other their disappointments, sorrow, aspirations, and expectations these are to be respected and any breach of confidence tears down the relationship.

Sometimes someone in the family assumes the ability

to speak for another member. Parents do it all the time. Someone asks a child a question, and before the child can possibly answer the parent is speaking for him or her. People like to speak for themselves; they want to be their own persons.

Most of us really are not comfortable being talked about even if the information is ever so good. For example, a child gets very good grades so the daddy makes it a point to tell this to friends in the presence of the child or in the child's absence. Or someone in the family may say, "Mom doesn't feel like going to the movie." Personal information is personal and should be shared only by the one whose information it is.

In our family we remember, and we forget. We repent, and we forgive, and begin again. Perhaps this is a rhythm in all family life, a pattern of love.

Looking at persons face-to-face is also a genuine expression of warm caring. Parents often punish children by denying them eye contact. I remember when Judi did something with which I was not pleased. As we moved about performing our tasks in the kitchen she said, "Mom, why won't you look at me?" I now wonder how I could have been so uncaring. Spouses often avoid eye contact as punishment. Is that difficult to confess? Looking directly into the eyes of another person pleasantly, perhaps with a smile, affirms that person's sense of worth. Unfortunately we sometimes reserve eye contact for making strong negative points, to give instructions or to reprimand. This may make young children obedient (only while they are young), but it does not make them feel loved. Members of the family may nurture each other emotionally by consistently giving eye contact.

In recent years persons have more openly admitted to skin hunger—the need for physical contact. The back doorbell rings. Bob walks in and says, "Give me five," as he slaps my open hand or his father's. That is followed by a warm bear hug. Bob needs physical contact. We all need to be touched, to be held, even as we need personal space and apartness. The family expresses warmth when members touch each other naturally. A grown-up son needs his father's arm around his shoulders as much as he needed his hair tousled as a little boy. Without embarrassment a mother may ask to have her neck or shoulders massaged. In the family that exudes warmth persons are touched and held and feel free to express their needs for appropriate physical contact with other members.

Claims are being made for the therapeutic value of laughter. Perhaps healing is helped by mirth as the scripture suggests: "A merry heart doeth good like medicine" (Proverbs 17:22). The Moffatt translation reads, "A glad heart helps and heals." I believe families cannot survive without laughter—quiet and robust and effervescent. Most families have their own jokes, their own rituals for making merry, and these are to be cherished and encouraged. Members of the family may be quite intentional in planning times of merriment—always being sensitive to the feelings of others. I do not think it is helpful to say to a disappointed or angry person, "Why don't you sing? It will make you feel better." Neither should someone in the family try to make a joke out of one person's distress until the discomfort has been fully shared and dealt with. Laughter is not a cover-up; it is a release and a celebration.

There are times when we just need to be present to another member of the family by listening or quietly sitting nearby. A sick child often doesn't want to talk, but feels comforted by having mother or father, brother or sister near. Grown-ups are similarly cheered, and in many situations all we can do is be quietly present.

In a caring family the joys and sorrows are shared in equal measure; all members feel enfolded. Children can hardly wait to get home to tell what happened. Half the fun of being chosen for the team is in sharing the news. Joy is doubled as it is shared, and sorrow is greatly diminished when a loving person absorbs part of it. Queen Victoria once wrote to Prince Albert: "You will find in that a proof of my love, because I must share with you everything that rejoices me, everything that vexes or grieves me, and I am certain you will take your part in it." In our family we are warmed as we share our joys and try to bear each other's burdens.

THE FAMILY PROVIDES LIGHT

The family provides light as it responds to the need caught up in the words, "Show me how to live." This need is expressed in many different ways. We all need guidance throughout our lives. Parents need to provide a great deal of guidance even as they gradually and consistently help their children to become self-reliant, independent, and capable of taking responsibility for themselves and others. Parents demonstrate a happy blend of authority and companionship. When direction is given it is simple, open, cordial, void of all arrogance. Parents are more than kind; they are kindly. When offering guidance they will find timing of the utmost importance. There is a proverb that relates to the importance of saying the right thing at the right time: "A word spoken in due season, how good it is" (Proverbs 15:23). But timing is difficult for parents. They are often aware that a child has deep concerns about some aspect of life and they are tempted to tell the child how to handle the situation before help is sought. Parents need to advise and counsel. Knowing when and how are difficult skills to acquire. Jan had a way of letting us help her think through things. After being out with her friends she would sometimes come in and sit on the foot of the bed and talk for a long time. Mostly she wanted me to listen, and that was easy because I knew she would make her own wise choices after she talked and thought through all the possibilities. In our family we have bumbled along and the children have been accepting of our frequent poor timing, perhaps because of the warm climate of the home.

While openness is an essential characteristic of a caring family, groundedness is no less necessary. Persons need roots, a sense of belonging. Spouses need to know each other's values as they grow and change. Children need to know the values of their parents. Parents abdicate their responsibility when they say they will not thrust any of their values or commitments on their children. Their philosophy is something like this: "We will expose the children to all kinds of ideas and experiences and when they are old enough they can make their own decisions, select their own values, and find their own direction." Of course, that is to be hoped, but unless children receive guidance and clarification in ethical, moral, and spiritual matters as children, they will be pitifully confused as they go out on their own. They will not be able to make mature judgments when they reach the age of maturity.

Testimonies are to be shared in the family. Sharing one's own experience and having family members respond often is a means of clarifying and evaluating where we are. For example, when I share what I have come to understand about God and life, I welcome my family's questions and comments. It helps the family understand me, and it helps me understand myself.

Storytelling has been an effective method of helping our family feel rooted. Grandparents tell stories of how it was when they were children—where they lived, how they traveled, what they played, the songs they sang, their customs and traditions. Parents share their stories with their children. Children are encouraged to tell their stories. I am sometimes amazed as our children tell theirs... our perceptions of past events are so different.

In guiding children we must be careful not to make promises or to hold out prizes. We should not offer too many hopes, too many choices, too much for too little. Instead we should encourage children to face life with faithfulness and determination. We may sometimes try to soothe and console too much when it might be more helpful to stimulate and motivate. We need to be strong. The family should brace us, revive us, invigorate us, put new heart and courage into us when we are dispirited, and enable us to snatch victory out of defeat. We meet the misfortunes of life with inspiration, and help each other be strong and live nobly.

THE FAMILY PROVIDES SECURITY

Life has been very gentle to me, yet there have been times when I have felt weak and alone, and in those times I have found strength and safety in my family. All of us experience fear and anxiety in greater or lesser intensity and we need a rod to hold onto. One day Rusty came home from first grade; the moment he got inside the door he began crying, and his whole body was trembling. After a bit he was able to tell me that the sixth grade boy who lived down the street had walked home with him and had told him the devil was going to get him (Rusty). The devil could come right through the bedroom window and some night he would grab Rusty out of his bed. (I don't know if he gave more details of what would happen after that or not.) Rusty's whole body was reacting to fear. I was glad I was home. We were able to bring warmth and light to bear on that experience, and Rusty gained a new level of security. He felt safe with his family in his home.

The story of the Norwegian-American family portrayed in *Mama's Bank Account* (the stage play, *I Remember Mama*) is a classic illustration of how "Mama" provided security for her children. The family growing up in San Francisco struggled constantly to make ends meet. In the face of any and all needs the resources were laid out and the children assured that if they had to they could draw on the bank account, but always they tried to avoid "having to go to the bank." It helped them through many difficult situations and each time Mama said, "Is *good*. See? We did not have to go down to the bank." Twenty years later Katrin took the check she received for her first story to Mama to deposit in the bank.

> Mama looked at me. "Is no account," she said. "In all my life, I never been inside a bank."
> And when I didn't—couldn't—answer, Mama said earnestly: "Is not *good* for little ones to be afraid—to not feel secure."

It is not good for anyone to feel insecure. The caring family provides security for all persons in it.

THE FAMILY PROVIDES SANCTUARY

The old saying about a man's home being his castle may need updating: "My family is my fortress." Surely there are times in every person's life when he or she needs to throw himself or herself into the arms of others. The family can be that place of refuge and protection, that place of privacy and peace, the place where masks can be removed and honest feelings shared.

OPPORTUNITIES FOR PASTORAL CARE IN THE FAMILY

Great events in family life are celebrated with pastoral caring—birth, death, marriage, baptism, and many other passages. The family rituals, the small and large ceremonies, the feast days provide opportunities for family members to express love and appreciation for each other. Caring is most apparent when important family decisions are made. At all times family members can carry the needs and concerns of other members of the family in their hearts for God's blessing. One sure way that God is in the world is by the loving care lived out by the people of God.

A lot of role modeling goes on in the family. Children learn the art and use of caring ways from parents, and parents learn caring ways from children. There are many interactions that teach us how we want to behave so that always we are learning how to be a family and how to care for each other in ways that will bring each and all of us to fulfillment. Yes, pastoral care goes on in the family with the shepherd's staff being passed around among family members. I believe the families of our children will be more nurturing than our family has been, and I believe this will be true for many families we know. The quality of each succeeding cycle will probably be richer. This gives me great hope and a sense of deep appreciation.

STUDY SUGGESTIONS

1. The author states that the "unique way in which love may be expressed in the family can be described as pastoral care." What are the unique ways that love is expressed in your family and in your church family?
2. The author speaks of Grandma providing her with ideas of family life. What has given you your ideas of family life? Try to make a list of your ideas and consider the origin of each.

      Ideas   **Origin**

3. The author shares beautifully how the pastoral care qualities of warmth, light, security, and sanctuary

have been lived out in her family life. How has each of these qualities been lived out in your family?

Ways Lived Out in My Family

Warmth:

Light:

Security:

Sanctuary:

PLANNING FOR COMPREHENSIVE CARE
by Pat Zahniser

What brought you into the Reorganized Church of Jesus Christ of Latter Day Saints?

What elements of church life are appealing to you?

Why have others joined you in this faith?

A majority of members will probably answer that the friendship and concern of the Saints was their first contact with the church. Initially, someone touched them. It was later that they developed a growing understanding of the church's doctrine. That "touching" was pastoral care. Its importance needs to be recognized and fully accepted by every member.

Developing a spirit of care for those around us and honing it to a fine edge will strengthen our membership and provide evangelistic opportunities far beyond our expectations. Pastoral care offered to those around us will not be self-serving if we also reach beyond. We can offer care and love to the inactive Saints, to friends of the church, and to our active church families. Christ called us to be the personification of his work; this is our mission.

The scriptures repeatedly speak of service to our neighbors as being our high calling. We are all familiar with the biblical concept of "Love thy neighbor" which is beautifully developed in the Book of Mormon: "When you are in the service of your fellow beings you are only in the service of your God" (Mosiah 1:49). This concept is further defined in the book of James: "Pure religion and undefiled before God and the Father is this, To visit the fatherless and widows in their affliction" (James 1:27).

In the past some have sought to make our primary mission that of baptizing new members after converting them to our doctrinal beliefs. Today we see the need to grow and expand more than ever, and it appears other options must be pursued to carry out our mission. New approaches could center around the development of a strong congregational base of pastoral care. Evangelism may take place as we reach out to care for the inactive members and friends of the church close to each of us, even those within our families.

THE CHURCH AS A "FAMILY"

The concept of the church as a "family" is shared by Saints everywhere. As a child I was taught that I belonged to a community of Saints—a church family. My parents taught that these people were much like our own family but the ties were the ties of faith. Thus I would respond with surprise and joy each time I "discovered" a Saint in a far distant place. My testimony is that this community concept is one of the most meaningful in Christ's church.

The idea of community was not just a peculiar interpretation my parents gave me. Rather, this concept has its roots reaching back into the earliest days of church history. Pioneer Saints sought to build communities under the Lord's direction. The theological implications of their efforts remain today. Two other aspects of our movement help to explain the prevailing idea that Saints are a family: (1) the persecution[1] suffered by the early members, and the reflection this persecution had on the personality of the church for years, and (2) the general attitude most members carry about the "rightness" of the church's mission. All of these factors help us understand the development of the unique "family" relationship between members.

WHY HAVE A PASTORAL CARE PROGRAM?

Today's Saints are experiencing the same problems that afflict friends of the church. (This was always true, but not always recognized.) Social institutions are eroding and this disintegration appears to be reaching inside the church. Yet a strong program of pastoral care can curb this erosion if the Saints will join together. Combative measures can be provided to assist people who are suffering through life's complexities. The goal of pastoral care is to provide strength through positive ministry.

The advantage a program of pastoral care has is that it serves both the members who provide aid and those who receive it. Pastoral care can move the church rapidly forward:

    a. Immediate and invigorated efforts should produce results for the mission of Christ. This mission,

restated by President Wallace B. Smith in the "Faith to Grow" program for the 1980s, *can* be accomplished through pastoral care and outreach.
b. Local members will gain strength through pastoral care programs, from which they will gain energy and spirit to move out into the community.
c. The church will fully care for its own[2] and still reach out to others.

Pastoral care may be provided individually or collectively within a congregation. There are many opportunities for both, and suggestions for each will be included in this chapter. Suggestions are general, since the size of the group, the makeup in ages and sex, and the particular areas of need will determine the kind of care given.

PREPARATION

Initial preparation calls for an adjustment in schedules in order to have time available to serve. Given the number of activities that assault us daily, including the activities we "must" and those we "want" to do, we must prioritize responsibilities. The question is simply, do we want to serve? The following suggestions may give some guidelines:

COMMITMENT: This is an absolute basic. If we are affirmative in our desire to serve, a solid commitment is necessary. We will serve when, where, and how we are needed as long as our strength and resources last.
—Our commitment may require us to organize a congregational pastoral care committee.[3]

—We must also accept the fact that we may have to work alone.
—Our commitment must be durable, steadfast, and Christ-centered.

PERSONAL PREPARATION: Prioritizing responsibilities has already been discussed. This involves time management.[4] We should set regular time aside on a consistent basis so our commitment does not slip away. In addition, we must be flexible enough to be available when emergencies arise.
—Preparation takes on less frightening aspects when we realize that our whole lives have been the training ground. The talents we have developed, the skills we have learned, the competence we have achieved on the job, and the management of duties at home and in church all provide the skills we need.
—Everyone has the ability to serve, but not everyone will recognize this or be willing to help. An understanding that our hands are all Christ has for his work may help us overcome feelings of inadequacy.

INDIVIDUAL PASTORAL CARE

Unless we know people, we cannot provide care for them. This is true of anyone we serve. The key word is *know*. It is far more than recognizing a face, being able to say a name, or engaging in small talk on Sunday mornings. Unless we really get to know those around us, our pastoral care will be as superficial as our "friendship" is.

—A peculiar trait of our human nature is that we try to keep our troubles within the four walls of our home. For that reason, we may be sitting in church next to people who are suffering silently. Since our friendship is only skin-deep we remain completely unaware of their needs. It is unlikely that this desire for privacy will change, so the solution lies in our becoming more aware. We must begin to build in-depth friendships.

—The consideration here is not to pry into the private lives of those close to us but rather to understand needs they might have and to offer our assistance. At this point it cannot be overemphasized that keeping confidences is absolutely necessary. It is essential in building relationships that we are seen as trustworthy. We must trust one another. Testimony services offer an opportunity to share together, to be open in seeking and receiving help from the caring people of the congregation.

—We need to develop an understanding about the difference between sharing information and gossiping and beware of the latter!

Deepened contact between people depends upon an atmosphere of risk-and-trust. We *risk* being knowing; we trust openness. Nothing necessary to the relationship can be withheld. Everything crucial to the relationship must be handled.[5]

How well do you know the members of your congregation? If it is small, you probably know everyone. If it is large, you may know most but not all. Try to answer the following questions, to see how well you *really* know them. Aim at ten out of ten:

1. Do you know what occupations the working members hold? Are you familiar with their job-related joys, concerns, and aspirations?
2. In families where both parents work, is it because of financial need? Do the parents have concerns regarding child care while they work?
3. What are the backgrounds of the members of your congregation? Where did they live originally? Why did they settle where they are now? How many years have they been in the church, and how did they happen to join?
4. Do you know the names and approximate grades (or ages) of the smaller children and youth? Do you know whose children they are?
5. If the children are grown, do you know where they are and what they are doing?
   (Note: These two questions are important, since many people regard their children as the most important thing in their life. Discussing their children is a great icebreaker for people you want to know better—but let them talk!)
6. Without being judgmental, do you have an idea about the strength of commitment of the members? This may show through their activity level, attendance, and expressed feelings about the local area and World Church. Are they in need of encouragement toward the work of the church?

Now the questions become more difficult and require some real soul-searching.

7. Do you know what day-to-day burdens the members carry? *Everybody carries at least one.*

8. If you are aware, what have you done to lighten the load?
9. Are you known in the congregation as one who will provide help in an emergency, or do the Saints leave you alone?
10. Have you found more meaningful relationships at work, at school, in the neighborhood or social groups than you have within the church?

A candid answer to the last question, like all the others, explains in part why the church needs to strengthen its members through pastoral care. Have you let yourself slowly be separated from your friends in the church?

> **Persons are created with the intent that they live not only as individuals but together in community. Unfortunately, however, persons experience alienation (i.e., separation) from many others in their immediate environment. Such separation is evidenced by overemphasis on personal well-being at the expense of the consideration of others. Very often we don't even know our immediate neighbors. People are also separated from themselves. They are unable to accept the fact that they are persons of worth and loved by God.[6]**

In strengthening one another, the Saints will also be able to strengthen the inactive members found in many church families and the close friends and relatives who have not yet associated themselves with the church. This caring and reaching out follows the instructions Christ gave to Peter: "When you are converted strengthen your brethren" (Luke 22:32).

COLLECTIVE PASTORAL CARE

Collective pastoral care generally takes the form of recreational gatherings, informal meetings, service and charitable projects. These gatherings provide an opportunity for members and friends of the church to become acquainted. Invite all the significant people in the lives of church members to attend. Do not allow these activities to become thinly disguised opportunities to try to convert or reactivate the guests. The gathering must be exactly what it purports to be. Evangelistic efforts may come later, but they will be dependent on the companionship members offer to the guests, and the movement of the Holy Spirit upon the lives of those individuals.

The advantage of planning an informal activity to which friends of the church are invited is the potential to help all participants become acquainted in a nonthreatening way. Other aspects that can make these activities especially good are as follows:

1. A wary nonmember spouse or friend is able to enjoy the company of the Saints in an informal setting. There may be no other time for this opportunity to discuss everyday concerns and to have fun together.

2. If the project is charitable in nature, members and friends of the church have an opportunity to work together for mutual goals.

3. The Saints can be observed by the guests, who will see they are normal, fun-loving, hardworking, and companionable.

4. Occasionally, friends of the church may be asked to carry the leadership roles in projects that might be in their area of expertise. This indicates to them that they

are accepted by other participants and expresses appreciation for their special gifts.

PASTORAL CARE AND "FAITH TO GROW"

The call to "grow" in the eighties means the need to strengthen one another—and this can be done through pastoral care. The call to "expand" means to evangelize—and this should be the natural outgrowth of pastoral care.

The strength of the church is the strength of its members. Pastoral care that leads Saints to help families unite can provide a vigorous new dimension to the church's mission.

Several years ago, a fine young woman who was active in her local congregation was approached by a nominating committee searching for a district woman's consultant. She was reluctant to take on this responsibility because her husband was a nonmember. She felt unable to serve and asked for additional time to discuss and consider it at home. Her decision came in the affirmative, upon the condition she and her husband had mutually agreed upon—all activities and traveling would be done together. As this good couple worked in the district, the friendship of the Saints was always offered unreservedly. When it was time for the children in that family to be baptized, the husband also gave his name. Today he works within his priesthood office. The pastoral care elements were all present in this illustration: companionship, concern, love, and the spirit of God working with this young couple and the membership. Had the Saints been reluctant to receive her offering because of her nonmember husband, the story might have been different. Today that district has four hard workers instead of one, and a joyous postscript is the beautiful experience of a family united in the faith.

PUTTING LOVE INTO ACTION

No rules can be written for individuals and groups providing pastoral care. Each person and situation is unique. The inner yearning to serve will help develop a sensitivity to the needs of others, and priorities will fall into place. Remember, pastoral care need not be an impossibility. It simply means putting love into action.

Several years ago, a helpful guideline was offered to the people of one active congregation. These people were concerned about one another and had made many efforts to provide all types of care. They were very responsive to one another's needs. Under the influence of the Holy Spirit, their presiding elder explained to them that when the "name" of an individual came to mind as they went about their daily work, it was the prompting of the Spirit—the still, small voice. They were admonished to respond immediately, not to turn it away. "Pick up the phone and call that person," he concluded.

Shortly afterwards, in response to this guidance, a young member telephoned an elderly couple who had been very active. Receiving no answer, she asked members living in the vicinity to check on them. They found the wife in bed, too ill to move, and her husband on the floor; he had suffered a serious stroke. While this couple never fully regained their health, they did live to worship with that congregation of friends again.

Not every telephone call will be that critical or that dramatic—but every call is needed. On the other extreme is a personal illustration. One day a short time ago I was feeling particularly low. The phone rang. It was one of my sisters in the church, calling to ask how I was. She said she had been thinking of me and wondering how things were going. This was nothing big...but how good it was to know someone cared enough to "touch" me.

The following illustrations of pastoral care indicate the scope that this service can take and show that ordinary people can provide extraordinary services:

—Stranded in a distant state for one week due to an auto accident, a young couple attended the local church. There they were taken in by the presiding elder's family who met all their needs. No qualifying questions were asked (e.g., membership, activity, priesthood). They were part of the family and a frightening experience for them turned out to be one fondly remembered.

—An ill, debt-ridden mother and three children, abandoned and left penniless by their husband/father, were brought food and help by congregational members. Ministry continued to be offered until the family was back on its feet.

—Planning to attend a men's retreat for the first time, two teen-age boys looked forward to spending the weekend with their father. Plans changed suddenly, however, when he came down with a bad case of the flu. Disappointed, the boys went alone. Several days later the parents of the two young men received a note from one of the district leaders, a humble man who always offered love to those around him. The note simply said how much he appreciated the boys' participation and contribution. Coming at a formative time in their lives, it undoubtedly affected the positive ministry they offer now.

—The mother of a large family returned home one evening and hurried her preparations to get dinner out of the way in order to spend the evening studying. She was a student and had just gone back to school some months earlier. A large casserole on the kitchen counter indicated someone had slipped in and out the back door. The note attached bore encouraging words of understanding about her work in college while still having children in school. Ironically, the gift was prepared for this family by an even busier mother! The pleasant evening meal expressed the spirit of that sharing.

—Just as the young couple returned home from the hospital and settled the husband into bed, the phone rang. "How much is your house payment?" The voice was that of a church member, a friend. Taken by surprise, the young wife asked him to repeat his question. "How much will your house payment be this month?" When she gave him the figure, he simply answered, "It's taken care of." The emergency surgery kept the young couple preoccupied with matters of health, and the nitty-gritty of daily living hadn't yet struck them. The man was self-employed and would have no income until he was back on the job. The perceptiveness and pastoral care of this good brother gave them a solution before they realized they had a problem!

—Loading a small group of young boys into his old car, a brother in the church shared his companionship with them. Coming from split-family homes, the boys looked forward to these days in the mountains or at the beach. There they played together, learned to work together, and, most important, learned what real Christian companionship could be. They learned to love the Lord. Today this man is well known for his singular interest in a particular area, but even when he was busy studying he did not let this deter him from offering pastoral care to these boys. He recognized the worth of persons and the nature of Christian love. His love may be measured today through the services offered by his "boys" as they reflect his caring attitude.

—On a winter evening, two church families received a call from a local government worker, also a church member. She was at the police station handling the care and placement of four young children whose father had left them and whose mother was on her way to the hospital after threatening suicide. A critical foster home shortage caused the worker to turn to her church for placement. Each family took two of the children and within two hours after her call they were settling into warm and friendly homes, unreservedly welcomed for an indefinite stay. The government officers and policemen were astounded at the speed and willingness to help that these church families demonstrated.

—Vacationing far from home, a middle-aged couple were caught in a small town when the wife fell very ill. She required immediate surgery and developed complications which kept her seriously ill for weeks. Although he rented an apartment, the husband spent most of his time at the hospital. It did not occur to either of them to contact the local church, possibly because they had been inactive in the preceding years. Aside from the medical personnel, their only contacts were with their children who were miles away. The church there was contacted, however, by a son who wrote a note explaining the situation to the presiding elder. Immediately, the couple were no longer alone. Church members visited the hospital, sent gifts, provided food, and met other needs. It was a long and difficult time for the couple—but one made easier when the Saints entered the picture.

—A young woman, mother of three very small children, found herself engulfed in ever deepening depression. Her concerns were the care of her children, the end (she thought) of a career in art, financial problems related to her house, and just depression in general. A neighbor, who happened to be a church member, made arrangements to introduce her to a retired member, a grandmother. The relationship between these two grew daily. The mother was allowed time to shop without fear of having to pay a sitter. At home, she had the companionship of this fine woman to help with the work and to visit about adult concerns. When her doctor suggested she begin therapy at the Family Mental Health Clinic, her new friend even accompanied her for the first visit. Improvement was slow but steady, and today the two remain the best of friends. Both are also giving vital service to the community through their particular gifts.

—One conscientious church couple have taken it upon themselves as part of their stewardship to keep members aware of good job openings. Not only do they personally share the information they collect, but they also assist in preparing résumés or letters of application. In a two-year period they have helped at least three members acquire challenging, well-paying positions. In addition, they have offered countless college students information on schools, financial aid availability, and help in filling out the numerous forms. Part of this service is a portion of the husband's position as a college adviser, but much of it is due to their desire to help their brothers and sisters in the church express their own gifts and talents to the utmost.

These examples[7] of pastoral care, with one exception, have been provided by people with no specific counseling or social work training. The skills they used included visiting, parenting, providing physical assistance in the form of food and transportation, and supportive services. In nearly every case, as much help was given as the providers were able to give, according to the needs they witnessed. In several situations their sensitivity caused them to know they were needed. None of the skills involved were extraordinary, but their application makes them unique and thrusts them into the realm of Christian service.

STUMBLING BLOCKS TO PASTORAL CARE

Providing pastoral care is not always without problems. Stumbling blocks will be encountered in many ways. Those you try to serve may resist. This underscores the need to make an approach that allows them to retain their pride and dignity. Some of the more common stumbling blocks are the following:

1. Some members feel that church people have no problems, or if they do, they have to be minor ones.

2. Other members feel that those Saints who do have problems brought them on themselves. They either did not live "correctly" or worship "righteously."

3. There is a rehash of the old cliché: "Saints have problems like everyone else, but Saints are able to cope. They just pray about it." What about the member who can't cope? Must each suffer alone? There is no shame in easing grief by sharing it with a friend; no weakness in talking out a decision. *The error lies in causing members to feel they must stand alone, because Saints are strong.* A true community of believers will offer strength to one another in times of sorrow and stress.

A different kind of hindrance to pastoral care service may be the size of the congregation. In small congregations where everyone is well known and where families go back for generations, efforts should be made to develop a Pastoral Care Commission whose aim is to reach inactive Saints, friends of the church, and active members. Larger congregations seldom have the problem of knowing everyone too well, but they fall into the trap of forming small cliques, locking others out.

This should be avoided, since everyone has ministry and gifts to share.

BEGINNING A PASTORAL CARE PROGRAM

In beginning the task of caring for the needs of congregational members, it may be difficult to find a starting place. These questions may provide a point of beginning:

1. Are there youngsters in your congregation who attend church alone? Are they living in a single-parent home? Are there children and teens who do not attend church at all? Could you "adopt" them by providing transportation and especially companionship?

2. Do you have senior citizens who are confined? Have you visited them and taken church-related materials (and maybe some good things to eat)?

3. Are you aware when members have short-term illnesses and need help for a day or so?

4. What is done for families in which the mother is sick? Are they helped out during that time?

5. Do widows, widowers, mentally retarded, or physically incapacitated members receive periodic visits from the Saints?

6. Do young families receive your offer to baby-sit occasionally, without charge?

7. Are hospitalized Saints assisted when they return home? Have you helped with their laundry, meals, cleaning, and errands during the convalescence period?

8. Who welcomes newcomers into the congregation? Have you helped them check out areas of the city,

including schools? Are they helped with the task of moving into their new home? Who assists them to find doctors, dentists, libraries, and grocery stores?

9. Do you provide ministry for members *away* from home (i.e., college students, service personnel, and people working on jobs that take them away)? Do they hear from the congregation through cards, letters, newsletters, or occasional boxes of cookies?

10. In relationship to Question 9, do those same members living in *your* area for a short time find themselves accepted as part of your family?

11. When death occurs within the congregation or among inactive Saints, do you assist in meeting the immediate physical and emotional needs of the family? Is this effort *sustained* until a kind of healing process takes place?

12. Are both parties of a divorce (among the membership) treated with respect? Do you avoid taking sides? Can you help the children through this traumatic period by offering them family relationships and recreation outside their own home?

13. Do recently retired members receive responsible church duties—particularly in the field of pastoral care? This not only takes up the slack from their recent job-related life-style but also provides the membership with their valuable contributions of experience.

14. Do you have an active, vibrant youth group, providing meaningful activities and wholesome recreation as outlets for teen-agers? Do you include these young people in your planning activities? They can bring great enthusiasm and vitality.

15. Does your congregation have a regular news-

letter? With proper organization, the cost and time involved will be minimal and the rewards will be great. Use it to publicize activities and services, news of members, and accomplishments of the Saints. It will bring members together! (Teens often enjoy working in this area, but let them do some of the "thinking" work, not just the assembling and sorting.)

PROVIDING AN ONGOING YEARLY PROGRAM

The foregoing suggestions call for individual or collective pastoral care. Collective activities, planned by the pastoral care committee, need to be directed toward the objective of strengthening the members and reaching out to friends of the church. Plan as many as your congregation can bear and alternate recreational gatherings with service or charitable projects. Consider gatherings of particular age groups alternating with those for mixed ages. Remember, this may be the only time church members really have a chance to become well acquainted, to achieve the goal of becoming a caring congregation and to reach out to others.

Most congregations already have a list of favorite gatherings. Here are a few more:

1. Carry-in dinners. These informal meals provide a minimum of work and a maximum of companionship. Plan them on a regular monthly basis, if possible. Each family brings one dish and one dessert (if desired). The congregation furnishes the drink and the glasses. Take turns setting up and cleaning up. For variety plan special times for inviting particular people (e.g., young mothers, senior citizens, children) and treat them as guests; have a celebration in honor of them. Carry-in dinners are a boon to young families and those living alone.

2. *Biweekly or monthly adult recreation.* Again, this is an easy plan to allow adults to share together in recreational activities. Begin by inviting all those over eighteen (and include singles) to the home of one couple who provide games and refreshments. The next gathering is planned by a couple who volunteer at the first meeting. From then on, all participants take their turns, and the gatherings move around continuously. An incredible variety of recreation can be provided, since the host couple or single person plans it. If the decision is to play miniature golf or something which costs, the people are responsible for their own expenses. (Note: Make a "No Children" rule and stick to it, except for some summer picnics. The group's purpose is for adults to get acquainted.)

3. *Adopt a couple.* An alternate method to the foregoing is to adopt a couple (where one is a nonmember or inactive Saint) and meet with the group once a month, saving the time in between to use socially with the couple. Go out to dinner, have them over to eat, visit and get to know one another.

4. *Special interest support groups.* Consider this for widows and widowers, divorced parents, singles, parents of teens, teens, families with terminally ill members, senior citizens, and grief groups. Meetings may be regular or sporadic according to the objectives of the group. A leader will be able to handle the special interest as long as it remains a support group with members sharing in uplifting one another. Do not attempt to provide professional counseling if you are not certified to do so. Invite guest speakers from the community, or move out into recreational pursuits if it is proper to do so. (Teens, senior citizens, widows, and divorced parents may find this enjoyable.)

5. *Crises committee.* If the congregation is moderately large, a committee made up of members who have gone through serious illness and death of loved ones is needed to provide immediate emotional support and ministry when those problems occur in other families. Stable, outgoing, optimistic Saints should be chosen or should volunteer for this sensitive ministry.

6. *Lay counseling.* If professional supervision and training are available, you may wish to establish a lay counseling program within the district or stake. Counseling can encourage and uplift everyone carrying a burden within the congregation's reach; it is an essential service for today's world. For more information on establishing a lay counseling program in your area, contact the Pastoral Care Office, the Auditorium, Box 1059, Independence, MO 64051.

7. *Holiday dinners, parties.* Plan these for the entire year so that a variety of entertainment is offered. Use all holidays, and—in-between them—plan other reasons to get together. Quality entertainment or recreation is necessary to keep the interest high.

8. *Congregational birthday parties.* Hold these once a year. Have all members whose birthdays fall in the same month sit together. Let them do their own table decorating and plan prizes for winners. Make the meal a carry-

in, so that primary planning can be spent on recreation and entertainment.

9. *Box socials.* These can make fund-raising enjoyable and serve other good purposes. For example supplant money with other items, such as IOU's for work. You can further change the old method by reversing it; have the men prepare the boxes to be bid on by the women.

10. *District, regional, or stake gatherings.* Nothing has been said about it yet, but yes, there *is* life beyond the congregation! Often this is overlooked, and enriching and enjoyable experiences will be missed if your congregation does not participate in these gatherings. When district, regional, or stake activities take place in your city, invitations to inactive members or friends of the church are in order. (You may have to lay groundwork for some gatherings, such as services of worship or business meetings.) If the gathering is held out of town, take a carload or a busload to it. The companionship and fun to be had as Saints travel to a workshop, retreat, or meeting should not be overlooked.

CONCLUSION

When planning for your pastoral care endeavors, especially those that are recreational in nature, remember that Saints love to be together. A meal, an evening of games, or other activity will be enjoyed. My testimony is that the personality of the Saints will be the dominant factor once your activity gets under way. And don't forget the more difficult service—that of aiding the bruised and broken.

> **Membership in the body of Christ does not make persons immune to hurt feelings or personal**

problems. The message and ministry of reconciliation must be made available to members and nonmembers alike.... *Pastoral care... is the responsibility of all the members of the body of Christ.*[8]

This is the call of Christ.

REFERENCES

1. "Persecution" is used here to help explain the problems with evangelistic growth the church has experienced in the past. Members were plagued with the ramifications from earlier persecutions that seemed to cause a churchwide "inferiority complex" which lasted for years. We began to break out of that complex during the past quarter of a century. Understanding how this early persecution affected the church helps us to see why there were no larger numbers baptized than were, and also how it caused the sense of community *within* the church as Saints clung together.
2. The intent is not to duplicate services already provided in the community; rather, pastoral care means the "management" of assistance to one in need. It matters not whether the services are provided by the church or the pastoral care provider taps local resources. The objective desired is to see that help is given in whatever form is needed, that sustained care is given, and that later follow-up service is offered.
3. An excellent article, "Establishing a Pastoral Care Commission," by Glen A. Campbell, appeared in the May, 1979, *Commission* magazine (page 25). It details the reasons for a commission and explains ways to set one up in a congregation.
4. Time management means organization. It also means minimizing the greatest time wasters—TV, long phone conversations, unnecessary shopping trips, poor quality reading material, and general disorganization of life-style. Time management means good stewardship. Time is a gift that all people—rich or poor—have; it comes in equal amounts to everyone to be used in a Christlike manner.

5. James B. Ashbrook, *Become Community*, p. 93.
6. R. Daniel Fenn and Peter Judd, "The Message of Reconciliation" in *Pastoral Care: The Fruit of the Spirit*, p. 15.
7. For additional, excellent examples of pastoral care, *To Serve with Love*, by Jo Montgomery, Herald House, 1974. For local services available to help people of the church, see *White Fields for Harvest*, by Deane Butler Edwards, Herald House, 1970. See also Barbara Howard's *Be Swift to Love*, Herald House, 1974.
8. Fenn and Judd, p. 25.

BIBLIOGRAPHY

Ashbrook, James B. *Become Community*. Valley Forge: Judson Press, 1971.

Campbell, Glen A. "Establishing a Pastoral Care Commission." *Commission*, May, 1979, pp. 25-26.

Commission, May, 1978. Entire issue.

Edwards, Deane Butler. *White Fields for Harvest*. Independence, Missouri: Herald House, 1970.

_____. *All Children Are Mine*. Independence, Missouri: Herald House, 1964.

Engstrom, Ted W., and R. Alec MacKenzie. *Managing Your Time*. Grand Rapids, Michigan: Zondervan Publishing House, 1967.

Fenn, R. Daniel and Peter Judd. "The Message of Reconciliation" and "The Congregation and Pastoral Care," *Pastoral Care: The Fruit of the Spirit*. Independence, Missouri: Herald House, 1975.

Howard, Barbara. *Be Swift to Love*. Independence, Missouri: Herald House, 1974.

Montgomery, Jo. *To Serve with Love*. Independence, Missouri: Herald House, 1974.

Yarrington, Roger. *Restoration Ethics Today*. Independence, Missouri: Herald House, 1963.

STUDY SUGGESTIONS

1. The author raised questions at the beginning of this chapter. After each question write in two or three answers. How do the friendship and concern of the Saints rank in your answers? Discuss your answers.

    What brought you into the Reorganized Church of Jesus Christ of Latter Day Saints?

    What elements of church life are appealing to you?

    Why have others joined you in this faith?

2. Does your congregation feel like a "family" to you? If so, what are the reasons for this? If not, what seems to be missing? What could be done to improve the congregational environment?

3. The statement is made that a program of pastoral care serves both the members who provide aid and those who receive that help. Discuss the implications of this statement.

4. In the section on "Becoming Acquainted—Really Acquainted!" the author raises ten questions for your consideration about the people in your congregation. How many of these questions can you fully answer? Begin now to start gathering the necessary information for you to become really acquainted with your congregational members.

5. The author states the importance of collective pastoral care occurring in the form of recreational gatherings, informal meetings, and service and charitable projects. List the various collective pastoral care activities your congregation planned during the previous year. Discuss the following questions in relation to the activities you listed:
   a. How was pastoral care shared in each activity?
   b. How did the activities enrich the congregational life?
   c. How did the activities relate to the evangelistic endeavors of the congregation?

6. The author shares many examples of pastoral care. Read through these together. Develop your own list of examples as you share together how people in your congregation have shown pastoral care to each other over the last year.

7. Stumbling blocks to pastoral care may present difficulties for your congregation. Discuss if the blocks the author presents will be problems in your congregation. Also, share any other blocks which may present problems.

8. The author shares numerous questions which can serve as a starting point for pastoral care in your congregation. Choose one or two of these questions and begin! After a week or two come back together and discuss your progress.

ISSUES IN PASTORAL CARE
by Myron Andes, Jr.

This chapter will deal with a collection of issues which deserve attention as pastoral care in congregations is considered. Each of the five topics is included in the belief that it is relevant to the experience of real people in actual situations as they seek to live as the body of Christ. Before these issues are considered, however, it will be helpful to examine briefly the understanding of *pastoral care* which underlies the discussion.

CARE

Caring is the art of letting other people matter. The word is sometimes used to refer to a feeling or emotional state: "I *care about* him." It can also have the more active meaning of giving care: "They *care for* their daughter's needs" These two senses—"caring about" and "caring for"—show the active and the feeling components which are part of what it means to care.

To say another person "matters" is to say that person has worth in and of himself or herself. To care is to recognize this worth and to act accordingly. This worth is independent of me, and my concern is therefore altruistic. When I care, I allow considerations of the good of the other to influence my actions. Caring is thus an intimate activity, for it means that the other person is to some extent taken into, and becomes a part of, my one, unrepeatable life.

Real caring cannot occur "on principle" or "in general"; it must happen in the specific instance of an individual person. It does not mean agreeing with the principle, "The worth of persons is great in the sight of God"; rather it means seeing and feeling the value and goodness in a particular person.

Everyone is in the process of growing, from the moment of birth until the time of death. To care is to be interested in someone's growth and devoted to promoting it. This promoting rules out trying to mold the person to a certain image we may have. It takes its cue from the person's own direction of growth and seeks to support and facilitate it, without determining for the other person the direction of growth. This recognition of a person's autonomy, along with the affirmation of the person's individual worth, shows a profound respect for both the person and the creative power that produced him or her.

Caring requires being present for others, sharing in their experience, seeking to understand it as if we were "inside their skin." We can come into direct contact with others only insofar as we are able to feel *with* them (not *for* them), to feel as if we *were* these other persons. Empathy is the skill of having and communicating such feelings of understanding for others, and is central to what it means to care.

Being interested in and devoted to another *for that other's own sake* can also be beneficial to us. It requires effort, risk, and possibly sacrifice, but in return it gives us a source of meaning and purpose in life. It also provides the warmth of companionship, which seems to be an important necessity for human beings.

PASTORAL

From early Christian times the church has been represented by the image of a flock. This image is what is referred to by the term "pastoral." The modern term which perhaps best conveys a similar meaning of a gathered, intimately interdependent body of individuals is *community*. In a true community, as in a flock, the interests and concerns of the individual members are connected. Each person cares about and for the welfare of the others. Ideally, the church is such a community.

The word *pastoral*, when attached to the word *care*, serves to limit the scope of discussion. It identifies the area of attention as those persons (and institutions affecting persons) that the *church* encounters. Though all care about or for someone (or something), the focus will be on the church's caring—that is, caring by those persons who make up the church community (or flock) for each other and for those with whom they, as the church, come in contact. Since our primary experience as the church is in *congregation*, we will center on caring within and by the congregation.

Any church community may be referred to as a "congregation." This includes local administrative units, but it also includes the larger "congregation" of the world church or even the greater Christian community. Perhaps, then, "pastoral care" may just as accurately be called "congregational care." Both of these terms refer to caring by members of a "congregation" for each other, and also for those whose lives the congregation touches. It means having these members and "others" matter enough to affect the very life of the congregation and those who share in it. It means the sharing of concern. It means sharing life.

In thinking about and seeking to promote congregational care, we find there are some issues which arise repeatedly. Five such topics will be examined in this chapter. The intent is to bring an awareness of the issues, so that they will be considered, discussed, and taken into account as persons work on pastoral care in their congregational life.

PLANNING VS. SPONTANEITY

Caring is often thought of as a feeling which arises as an automatic response to certain stimuli such as helplessness or "cuteness." Yet for care-giving to be effective, there must often be an element of planning and preparation involved. Planning and spontaneity may be seen as conflicting but equally necessary factors which must constantly be kept in balance in a successful pastoral care program.

Without a "welling up" of human emotion, there can be no real caring. Sympathy, empathy, concern, and appreciation are some of the labels given to feelings which prompt us to care for another person. We may then express our caring in words or concrete actions. From experience, each of us knows that the very same words which are at one time rich in meaning will at another time, if not accompanied by the appropriate emotion, seem empty and hypocritical. The words, "I love you," may become hollow and habitual, or they may be very alive and meaningful, depending on the feeling which accompanies them or is lacking.

Expressions of concern which arise spontaneously are unplanned and genuine. Sometimes congregational activities and programs may become so structured and routine that they lose the effectiveness which goes with true concern. Some persons may then experience "the church" as being cold, empty, mechanical, or hypocritical.

An example may well be the traditionally organized priesthood visiting program. This has proved to be quite meaningful to many people in many situations. In some congregations, however, great difficulty is experienced in carrying out such a program. Little enthusiasm may be felt for the program by those visited and/or by the visitors themselves. Yet great success has come in some jurisdictions from impromptu, unscheduled visits by priesthood, priesthood and spouses, or others. These visits, which occur for a natural reason and arise out of a real concern, can at times render more ministry than an official priesthood visit. They will also tend to occur at the appropriate time, when the need or opportunity is apparent, and not just according to a schedule.

Such spontaneous expressions, however, suffer one severe drawback: they are not consistent. There is no guarantee that someone will perceive a need and initiate a visit when it is needed. If pastoral care is left entirely to such "chance" activities, there will undoubtedly be many needs in the congregation which will go unnoticed and unmet. With such an inconsistent system, people often wonder why, in a group which speaks so often of love and service, no one knows their hurt or their joy or seems willing to have them share it.

It would be nice to think that members of the fellowship were so concerned and so in touch with one another that pastoral care needs would take care of themselves. Such a view, however, is hardly realistic. It is for this reason that programs must be planned and opportunities created for caring and loving fellowship to take place.

Very little that we do occurs without planning, in pastoral care or any other area of endeavor. A counselor and a client seeking help arrange a time when they can meet. Two families plan to have a picnic together. A congregation organizes a potluck farewell for a family that is moving away. All of these examples show planning for caring. Yet if these activities become merely a matter of course, something other than caring takes place. The traditional gold watch given at retirement can become simply an expected trinket, when it originally was intended as a sincere token of gratitude, respect, and esteem.

Another example is a congregation near a large university which set up a "Town Parent" program. Local families volunteered to provide opportunities for students newly away from home to share in a family setting from time to time. A similar arrangement developed on its own in another college town between one student and friends of her family who happened to live nearby. There were probably many other students at this college who would have benefitted from such an arrangement, but there was no program planned to provide for it. The friendship which did develop, however, was highly satisfactory both to the family and the student, perhaps because they did it out of their own mutual needs and desires. At the university congregation with the organized program, not every pairing of students and "town parents" was effective, since the need for it was not always present. Yet the program did ensure that such ministry was available when it was needed, and some people benefitted from it greatly.

It appears, then, that spontaneity is necessary to make pastoral care real, and the program must be flexible enough to meet situations as they occur. Planning is needed to provide reasonable consistency and assurance that needs will not be overlooked or go unmet.

This tension between planning and spontaneity is well recognized in the Christian message. Jesus told the parable of the talents (Matthew 25:14-30), emphasizing accountability for the use of resources and their investment in the future—*planning.* Yet he also spoke of "taking no thought for the morrow" (Matthew 6:25-34). The concept of stewardship includes the intentional management of those resources which have been made available to us, including time, abilities, material things, effort, and concern. It thus involves a conscious planning of ministry. But we are also called to minister to persons at the point of their need, and that need may not be known in advance. The Good Samaritan did not plan his act of kindness ahead of time; rather, he responded to the need in the situation, spontaneously reacting out of the goodness of his heart. It is good for us to remember that both of these styles of ministry are affirmed in our scriptural heritage, and that we need to make use of both in our personal and congregational life.

In order to help promote a healthy balance between these two poles, a congregation can do several things. First, it can identify certain typical, recurring pastoral care needs within its fellowship and plan programs to meet them. What these are will depend to a large extent on the particular makeup of the congregation in terms of age, marital status, occupations, education, and other factors.

Second, it can establish some sort of feedback network to help make known needs and opportunities for pastoral care. This could include such organizational features as pastoral groups, visiting programs, or other means of discovering and reporting concerns (always respecting the individual's privacy). At least one congregation has used the Wednesday evening service effectively by allowing opportunity for participants simply to share publicly what is going on in their lives, in such areas as job and school. The size of attendance at the services indicated that such a means of sharing was both desired and meaningful.

Third, the congregation can promote and provide opportunity for spontaneous pastoral care. This function can be partially served by the feedback network already mentioned. Beyond this, shared experiences such as picnics, hikes, workdays, and game nights allow informal caring ministry to be expressed in a supposedly "nonreligious" setting and also help participants to know better the needs, concerns, and joys of one another. These could take place as an activity for the entire congregation or for a smaller group.

Fourth, the congregation can include in its educational program studies about pastoral care, stressing among other things the need for both planned ministry and spontaneous response.

And fifth, worship services and other aspects of congregational life can reflect concern for persons and their needs. Each of the ordinances serves as a symbol and as a vehicle for ministry to personal needs. Care may be taken to emphasize these meanings in the sacraments, and other aspects of congregational worship may be designed to further serve pastoral care needs. Opportunity may be given not only to consider or discuss pastoral care but also to practice concern in very specific ways. Every facet of congregational life provides the opportunity for promoting or detracting from the caring spirit of community. By creatively utilizing these opportunities, the congregation will be sharing in the divine concern for individuals and their needs.

The goal for programs and activities should be to render effective Christian service because of real concern. If caring is honestly not present in a particular activity it will be hollow, and there is no reason to waste time and effort continuing it until the concern can be generated. If concern does exist but it cannot be effectively expressed or implemented, careful planning and perhaps education may be needed to enable God's people to serve with love.

In short, the congregation can plan to meet known pastoral care needs and develop programs to facilitate spontaneous expressions of pastoral care. But no amount of planning can replace the real and responsive feeling of authentic caring. And no amount of goodwill can assure that pastoral care needs are consistently recognized and met. A good pastoral care system must have a workable balance between planning and spontaneity.

SELF-CARE VS. CARE FOR OTHERS

Another balance needs to be maintained between care for others and self-care. "Self-care" refers to attention paid to one's own needs, to treating one's self as well as one treats others. Overemphasis on either of these aspects of pastoral care to the exclusion of the other can lead to serious problems for individuals and for the church.

Service to others is an important part of the Christian gospel. In fact, the servant may be seen as the central image of Christian belief. Jesus is recorded as having said, "Whoever would be great among you must be your servant, and whoever would be first among you must be your slave" (Matthew 20:26-27). The demand of our faith is indeed to show love for others in our actions.

John 15:12-13 is often used as the measure of the extent to which a Christian ought to go in carrying out the servant role: "This is my commandment, that you love one another as I have loved you. Greater love has no man than this, that a man lay down his life for his friends." Such willingess to give of one's self on behalf of others was surely shown by Jesus. It has been lived out by many others also, both in dramatic ways and in small, unnoticed sacrifices. To deny one's own desires to benefit a fellow human being is perhaps the most noble capacity of the human spirit.

The commandment to lay down one's life for one's friends has, however, been interpreted by some as a call to live a life of complete and continual self-sacrifice and self-denial. Such disregard for the self is a misinterpretation of the meaning of the gospel. Jesus is also recorded as saying, "You shall love your neighbor *as yourself*" (Matthew 22:39, italics added). This would indicate that we ought to love ourselves also, to have respect for ourselves as creatures of God. If it is true that "Men are that they might have joy" (II Nephi 1:115), then this statement must apply to *all* persons, including us. This would make it as evil for us to neglect the care of ourselves as to ignore another in need. The affirmation of the gospel is the worth of *all* persons, including ourselves.

Examples of such lack of self-respect are all around. They are the people who become so involved in church activities (attending meetings, serving on committees, printing bulletins) that they wear themselves out to the point that they can no longer enjoy life. They are those who give of themselves (time, money, effort, emotional concern) until there is nothing left. They expend their entire reserve of resources and eventually become "burnt out." This is all done in the belief that it is their proper "Christian service" or sacrifice. Such people will often "drop out" completely after their period of intense giving, feeling empty and unfulfilled. They may come to the point of wondering, "When is someone going to do something for me?"

What is required to avoid such a result is a healthy sense of "stewardship of the self." We are called to exercise wise stewardship over all we can influence. And where do we have more influence than over our own lives? Perhaps our serving of others should begin with maintaining ourselves in a condition in which we are able to give. We must evidence in our own lives a joy and zest for living before we can expect to bring these things to others. The best gifts in life are shared, not given away.

It is unrealistic to deny that we have needs just as anyone else has. If others need occasional assistance and time apart for spiritual uplift, then so do we. To live Zionicly means to live in *mutual* support, serving and being served by each other.

To go to the opposite extreme, however, and become preoccupied with ourselves is a danger to be avoided. Meeting our own needs, or pursuing self-fulfillment, may become an excuse for self-centeredness, an escape from responsibilities to others. What is needed is a balance, a regard for self as equally important as others, but not more important.

All that has been said here in regard to individuals applies to the church. Some congregations may become so involved in "community service projects" that their own needs for spiritual uplift are neglected and all their resources expended. Probably more frequent, however, is a congregation which becomes self-centered and ingrown to the point that there is no outreach or service at all. This happens when we become so concerned with our own needs and desires (programs, building improvements, a new organ) that we do not recognize the needs of those to whom we are sent to minister. We may succeed in maintaining ourselves, but we do not become the servants we are intended to be.

Keeping a balance between self-care and service to others is a constant challenge for individuals and congregations. We must keep ourselves and all of our resources in a condition in which we are able to be effective servants. And we must be able to enjoy life if we are to share that joy and "good news" with others. We can teach others that they are worthwhile and valued by God only if we value ourselves and offer ourselves to them. Pride may thus be balanced with humility, self-worth matched with worth of others, and the maintaining of our own well-being combined with a recognition of the claim of others upon us.

EDUCATION FOR PASTORAL CARE

If a congregation is to grow in the area of pastoral care, a first step is the education of its people. Since pastoral care is the task of all members, all will benefit from some sort of learning to help them with their responsibility. This includes children, youth, and adults of all ages; male and female; priesthood and nonordained persons; all occupations; and members of all theological leanings.

As with any other training, pastoral care education involves three types of learning: knowledge, skills, and attitudes. All who are involved in ministry to others need some of each of these to function well in their special calling. Each person already has some background in these areas, whether it is realized or not. The role of pastoral care education is to increase understanding, to teach new skills and sharpen old ones, and to foster a caring attitude.

Knowledge. It is inconceivable that one could deeply care for persons or be effective in helping them without having some degree of understanding of their situation and needs. In any given congregation or community there is a wide variety of persons. Each individual is unique, yet there are certain universals which apply to everyone, and certain similarities among people which indicate natural groupings. Learning about these individual, group, and corporate needs is the responsibility of pastoral care education.

Certain circumstances give rise to special problems and special opportunities. Single parents, young families, newly retired persons, adolescents, and "midlifers" all have characteristic needs for special types of pastoral care ministry.

Researchers have discovered much about the different stages of life and how to cope with them. Much is also known about the process of dealing with special circumstances such as death, divorce, or mental illness. Of course, one should not expect to produce a congregation of expert sociologists, psychologists, or theologians. Much of this knowledge involves specialization, and it is unreasonable to expect all members of the congregation to learn all of this. A few may undertake specialized training to serve the whole body in a particular way (e.g. becoming lay counselors). Still, some insights have broad application and can be readily acquired by anyone. For example, obtaining a basic understanding of the life cycle and the developmental tasks of childhood, adolescence, middle age, and old age is a realistic and worthwhile objective. Understanding the grief process, or the pressures of building a career or adjusting to a new marriage are within the range of possibility, and even responsibility, of a caring congregation.

Skills. Good intentions and theoretical knowledge have one thing in common—they are necessary; but this is not sufficient to produce good results. For pastoral care to be effective, a caring attitude and sound understanding must be matched by the ability to *do* what is needed. Teaching the skills for implementing pastoral care is an easily neglected but essential part of a good pastoral care program.

Such skills range from those anyone can learn and use, such as good listening skills, to highly specialized counseling skills. The educational opportunities a congregation makes available and individuals pursue depend on the needs, resources, and interests present. Knowing what skills to develop will depend on having developed already a loving understanding of the needs to be met.

Skills seem to be particularly hard to develop in a church setting. The reason, perhaps, is that skill learning requires practice and application (doing something). We are in the habit of sitting and receiving at church, which is more suited to attitude and knowledge learning. Yet our timidity and inertia must be overcome if we are to become effective servants. We need to become active learners, for without skills to serve we shall become "as sounding brass, or tinkling cymbals."

Pastoral care deals with real concern for the real needs of real people. Such ministry requires caring, understanding, *and* skilled response. Education, in the church or otherwise, may be used to support each of these requirements, enabling us to become more effective ministers of God's love.

Attitude. As mentioned in the first section of this chapter, a caring attitude is essential to personal ministry. Although an attitude cannot, perhaps, be taught, it can be "caught." Preparation for such ministry can involve sharing with other persons who are deeply caring, since true concern seems to be contagious.

Also, an environment can be created (through worship services and other means, as well as classes) which will deepen and expand the caring already present in each member. Ways may be found to inform the congregation about needs of which it has not been aware, in the world at large, in its own community or among its own members. Activities may be used that bring a greater understanding of needs that are already known.

The spirit of Christ lives among those whose love is ever growing and expanding, widening and deepening. It is characterized by an increasing sensitivity to the meaning of our shared life and to the feelings and experiences of others.

PLURALISM

We live in a pluralistic world—that is, differing views, opinions, and ways of life exist side by side. They differ and sometimes clash; but no one system or idea has become universal, nor is one likely to do so. This is what we face in the world at large, in the World Church, and within congregations. Such a situation puts us in tension—a tension of old and deep-rooted values, of alternative ways of handling differences. These stem from perhaps the very basis of what it means to be a human being.

As human beings we are able to think and to feel. We all *believe* certain things—about what is real, what the world is like, what is valuable, and how to live. The most important of our beliefs are tied up with what we think about God. Many of these beliefs are instilled in us by our parents and others born before us. Usually we are taught them directly, or indirectly, through the institutions of our culture, but some we come to more or less on our own.

Part of what it means to believe something is that we are willing to stand up for it and therefore to stand against whatever opposes it. It is really not possible for us to think that we are wrong, for if we do we can no longer believe as we did and must adopt another view. If I think that one of my ideas is wrong, it is really no longer my idea; I have changed my mind. We are able to act only as if what we believe is true, which means that whatever conflicts with what we believe is false. Our natural dedication to things that are important to us implies resistance to anything different.

Yet as human beings, we are also social by nature. We must get along with other people and other groups, some of whom will certainly not be exactly like us. Enabling us to live together is the ideal of toleration. Respect for the fact that others have as much right to their opinions and beliefs as we do to ours gives rise to a certain humility. After all, unless everyone could agree on one standard to measure truth or right, there is no mutually acceptable way to judge between different beliefs. We may make legitimate appeal to the "testimony of the Spirit," but when others have conflicting "testimonies" which they also claim are "from God," our problem of finding a standard that everyone can accept is not solved. The same is true of appeal to scripture and other "authorities."

Religious toleration, "peaceful coexistence" among nations, and the ability of members of different political parties to live next door to each other are all examples of successfully handling pluralism. Most of us soon learn that it is possible to become close friends with others whose views are radically different from our own.

These two basic attitudes toward differences are very much in tension—"standing up for our beliefs" and toleration of different beliefs and ways of life. Certainly some extremists have believed that they had all of the truth and have sought to eliminate all alternative views. They have given rise to some of the worst tragedies in human history. Oppositely, some people are so "flexible" and "accepting" that they do not stand for anything.

These attitudes toward diversity become apparent as people approach differences in culture, subcultures, and ethnic groups. They also show up when encountering differences of opinion on political, moral, or theological matters. They apply to strongly held notions about the mission of the church, church policy and practice, and basic ideas concerning the meaning of the gospel.

Our scriptural record includes both of these attitudes. The apostle Paul admonishes both to "stand fast in the faith" (I Corinthians 16:13) and to "prefer one another in love" (Romans 12:10). More recently, we were told

"The spirit of unity must prevail..." and "the apostolic council...are directed to interpret...the gospel in a manner appropriate to the circumstances in which they find...persons" (Doctrine and Covenants 150). Those involved in ministry in cultures new to the church are discovering the need to let persons express the unique meanings of the gospel for those cultures. At the same time it is becoming evident that the church can move forward only if it is united.

These conflicting principles of steadfastness of conviction and toleration of diversity operate throughout our life experience. On the congregational level, many feel that effective ministry is prevented by differences among members. Yet it is also evident that there is no way to get everyone to agree entirely, and even if it could be done it would rob the congregation of much of its vitality and lead to a one-sided view of things.

Our task is to affirm something which gives meaning to life without becoming dogmatic, to be accepting of divergent views and practices without losing all moral and rational guidelines.

This problem has application to pastoral care because it has to do with how we deal with and minister to people. We rightly wish to stand in support and testimony of those things we believe to be true and right. We want to convince others to agree with us. This is part of what it means to stand for something. Yet this tendency needs to be tempered by a respect for the other persons we encounter. They have as much right to their views as we have to ours. We must, in addition to having the courage to stand by our convictions, have the humility to realize that we just might be wrong. And in any case, we must respect the agency of others enough to accept them and their views.

Jesus was not timid about sharing his beliefs and values with people. He did not shrink from accusing the Pharisees or clearing the temple. Yet his manner was most often forgiving and understanding. He stood up for what he believed by loving his enemies as he lived and as he died. He struck his own peculiar balance on this issue, and we must each strike our own.

Another question which applies to persons who have proclaimed loyalty to a group such as a church, political party, or country could be expressed in this way: "How much difference of opinion can be tolerated before I must say 'Either they go, or I go'?" This becomes a very real question when differences arise on important matters, such as how to spend resources, what to teach, and how to conduct services of worship.

Some groups have attempted to solve this problem by identifying a core of "doctrine" which serves as a measure of who is "orthodox" and who is "heretical." Our church has not chosen to be so legalistic. As a result, it has a rich variety of opinions, theologies, worship styles, and life-styles. Without such a creed, however, we must each decide for ourselves the meaning and depth of our commitment and the reason for identifying with this body.

As we seek ways to live together in a pluralistic setting, conflicts will necessarily develop. Some guidelines for handling these are considered in the next section. Certainly we must find ways through the conflicts to offer what is meaningful to us, while respecting those who differ from us.

CONFLICT RESOLUTION

Conflict will arise in any group. Since different people have different needs, desires, and understandings, they will inevitably conflict. In fact, within any individual there are contradictory needs and wants, which give rise to internal strife.

This means that conflict is a natural and necessary part of life. Yet as a rule we view conflict as bad and avoid it at almost any cost. Human beings have developed a wide variety of ways of coping with conflict, including ignoring it, pretending it does not exist, always giving in to avoid a confrontation, distracting attention to another subject, appealing to an authority for a solution, and bullying their way through to attain their own desires without regard for others. While each of these may be appropriate in certain situations, there is an alternative which in most cases is more fitting to an attempt to live together according to the gospel of Christ.

Christianity is, at its heart, an extremely ethical religion. Central to its beliefs is the obligation to consider others: "As you wish that men would do to you, do so to them" (Luke 6:31). This makes us responsible as Christians for doing not only what we want to do, or what we think is right, but also for giving equal consideration to other people and acknowledging their claim on us. In the event of conflict, then, we are obliged to try to find a solution acceptable to all—not a compromise everyone can "put up with" but a solution with which everyone involved is truly satisfied.

Such a solution may not always be possible. Chances of finding one are enhanced, however, by a high degree of trust between the disputants. If one is opposed by a stranger, or one who it is assumed would take unfair advantage if possible, then a meeting of minds is highly unlikely. Known and trusted friends, however, who can be depended on and who know that the other cares for them, are much more likely to reach a satisfying conclusion.

In the church we sometimes become alienated from one another by labeling, categorizing, and splitting into factions. This promotes seeing the "opposition" in a dispute as separate from us and leads to distrust and suspicion of motives. Remembering that we are all together, one body in Christ, promotes trust in the sincerity of those in disagreement and the acknowledgment that they do so in good faith out of honest conviction and concern. This evidences the respect for the worth of persons which was proclaimed, taught, and lived out by Jesus.

Thus, for example, when someone wishes to change a traditional order of worship or opposes a new program or material, there are two basic types of response. We may think in terms of opposing groups, with one "side" being "right" and the other as "fighting against God" or "subverting the gospel." Or we may see all as part of one body, honestly seeking to serve to the best of their abilities and understanding. The latter approach entails trust as a basis from which to work; the former has no such basis and must end in a power struggle.

There are various techniques for resolving interpersonal and group conflicts, but the foundation common to any such process is trust and faith in those with whom one is in disagreement. This foundation is laid through sharing together in many activities over a period of time. As people work and play together they learn about one another in a way for which there is no substitute. This may make it possible to understand what there is in a person's background, experience, or way of thinking which leads him or her to take a certain position. But, most important, it develops an interest, and to some extent, an investment in that person—who is considered not an opponent, but a friend who disagrees.

Very seldom do we deliberately set out to do "something bad." Rather, we have differing ideas about what is good. Knowing the people in the congregation (or other setting) enables us to realize in times of conflict that our opponents do not have evil intent but other ideas of what is good. This is the basis on which a resolution can be made.

Differences of opinion can be easier to handle when persons are encouraged to share together in non-threatening ways. The better people are able to get to know each other and the more they do together, the greater the trust that can exist among them, and the more they can care for each other. Such trusting and caring provide a necessary starting point in resolving conflicts when they arise and may also reduce the number of conflicts. These are the central qualities by which a relationship is identified as Zionic.

CONCLUDING THOUGHTS

Pastoral Care, conceived as concern for the needs of persons, is a natural and simple activity. We all have the "instincts" for it, inasmuch as we care about others.

Everyone is capable of being concerned for, respecting, and sharing in the lives of other persons. Yet the details of actually carrying it out are sometimes very complex.

In this chapter five basic considerations have been offered to keep in mind as we face the challenge of meeting the pastoral care needs of those with whom we come in contact. It is hoped that these brief comments will stimulate more thinking, reading, and discussion in this area.

STUDY SUGGESTIONS

1. The author defines caring as "the art of letting other people matter." Discuss the implications of this statement. What is your reaction to this definition?
2. The author describes the focus of pastoral care as being the church's caring. What does he mean by this? What is your reaction?
3. The author discusses in length five issues relating to pastoral care in congregational life.

   Planning vs. Spontaneity
   Self-Care vs. Care of Others
   Education for Pastoral Care
   Pluralism
   Conflict Resolution

Have five persons (or small groups) give a report on each of these issues. The report could include (1) a brief summary of what the author says, (2) a reaction statement by the reporter (or group), and (3) an analysis about how the issue is being handled and can better be handled in your congregation. After each report is given, time should be provided for all to have an opportunity to share their opinions.

PASTORAL CARE AND PRIESTHOOD RESPONSIBILITY

by A. Bruce Lindgren

Pastoral care is often seen as a priesthood responsibility in spite of the fact that it is frequently carried out by persons who are not ordained. The women's department and youth groups, for example, are often involved in a good deal of pastoral ministry through their contacts with church members and friends. Much care also comes about when people call on their personal friends within the church to help them with special needs or problems.

Still, pastoral care is often associated with the responsibilities of priesthood. There are probably two major reasons. First the presence of the priesthood in the church is a *symbol* of the church's concern for persons. Second, priesthood members in a local congregation are called to *function* in ways which provide pastoral care. To understand this situation, we need to examine the nature and function of priesthood ministry.

Ministry, in its fullest sense, is the responsibility of the entire church. All of us who have taken upon ourselves the name of Christ are called to represent him in all of our relationships with other persons. Ministry is nothing more (and nothing less) than relating to others in the way Christ would relate to them. In this sense, then, all members of the church perform ministry, and all members of the church are called to represent the Christ.

The ministry of priesthood is a special function of this larger ministry of membership. Experience tells us that many tasks may be ignored if they are left to a large group. Pastoral care is a good example. As individuals in the church, we may receive help from others when we need it, and we may offer a caring ministry whenever we see a need. Yet we do not always recognize all the needs of every person in the congregation. Many may have needs for pastoral care which are not met if we simply say that we receive pastoral care on an informal basis from all members of the church.

There is a need, then, for persons who are specifically called and/or designated to offer specialized forms of ministry such as pastoral care. In fact, we can say that there is a need for persons who are called to offer particular kinds of pastoral care. That is, pastoral care is a fairly broad term which refers to a wide range of individual and family needs, and ministry should be appropriate for the specific kinds of needs which occur. Members of the priesthood are called from the congregation to meet some of these specific needs. They are to minister "according to the gifts and callings of God" (Doctrine and Covenants 17:12a). In a congregation, the branch president or presiding elder is specifically charged with the task of calling persons with particular gifts and talents to appropriate priesthood offices under the guidance of the Holy Spirit.

A call to a priesthood office is a call to service rather than a call to privilege. Therefore, priesthood authority is a call to responsibility rather than a call to a place of honor from which others are excluded. With the exception of administering the ordinances and sacraments, there are few tasks which are exclusive to priesthood in a congregational setting.

The area of pastoral care is an obvious example. Several members of a congregation may be ordained to the offices of deacon, teacher, priest, and elder. All who hold these offices have special responsibilities and callings in the area of pastoral care. Yet many members in the congregation may also exercise this function.

WHAT IS PRIESTHOOD MINISTRY?

Priesthood ministry in pastoral care is unique in that it is carried out by those who have been specifically called to meet particular needs on behalf of the entire church. This may be seen in several ways.

First, priesthood ministry is one indication that the church desires to provide care on an intentional and systematic basis. Certain kinds of needs must be met "on the spot" by the person available to provide ministry. A child, for example, may provide comfort and support for a friend who has just been ridiculed by an older brother or sister.

Unfortunately, there is not always someone present in times of need. Older members of a congregation may feel out of place. Inactive members may be cut off from contacts within the church through which they might receive ministry. Parents of young children may become so hurried with the many responsibilities of daily life that they do not take time to develop relationships which might be supportive in times of crisis. In each of these cases, there is a need for the church to reach out in an intentional way to provide care for those who might not otherwise receive it. The presence of priesthood ministry is one symbol of such outreach.

Second, priesthood members are "caring" rather than "political" officers. Most organizations have officials designated to be "in charge of" their programs. This is necessary if an organization is to maintain some sense of direction, but those who are leaders must be concerned about the organization as a whole. Thus, the concern of the organization for individuals can suffer. In the church, one way this tendency is countered is through the priesthood. Members of the priesthood represent the church as a whole, yet they are called primarily to care. They are, in a sense, officers who are called to be especially concerned that individuals and families are not lost in the church's attempt to carry out a program. They are called to help keep the church's concern for its overall program in balance with its concern for individuals and families.

Third, priesthood provides the church with the means to meet specific needs of individuals and families. Every individual and family has particular needs which may or may not be similar to the needs of others. When the church meets together as a body, it is not possible to meet every need of the people present. For example, if a worship service is focused on the theme, "Stewardship of Time," many persons may be helped. Yet some individuals and families may have circumstances in their lives which make it difficult for them to exercise good stewardship over their time. For them specific help may be needed. Others in the congregation may have other needs which are more pressing at the moment than the stewardship of time. Someone should be available to meet the particular needs which they have.

Priesthood is one way in which the church can minister to people with widely varying needs. Just as there are many needs, there are also many people with gifts and abilities to meet them. Some are particularly good counselors. Others might be able to help families manage their finances more effectively. Still others can be helpful in the area of personal and family worship. Ordination is one way in which the church can commission some of its members with unique talents and abilities to minister in a personal way to the variety of needs which exist.

Priesthood ministry in pastoral care, then, is a concrete symbol of the commitment of the entire church to care for those within its fellowship. All members of the church are called to offer pastoral care according to the gifts of God to them. This call is underscored by the calling of specific persons to specific offices through the structure of priesthood. The authority of priesthood with regard to pastoral care is the authority to care and the authority to serve others in an exemplary way.

THE FUNCTION OF PRIESTHOOD

The offices of deacon, teacher, priest, and elder carry the major responsibility for priesthood ministry in the local congregation. Although persons holding other offices may be involved in the congregation's activities, the focus of their ministry is often directed into other areas of the church's life. Each priesthood office in the congregation has its own function and purpose.

Deacon

The deacon is called to lead and teach a life of service and commitment and to affirm the worth of each person. This call can be expressed in many ways. When the church gathers for worship, for instance, the deacon often greets persons as they enter the church, helps them find a place to sit, and makes sure that the sanctuary is comfortable and orderly. While this provides decorum, it is also an expression of pastoral care. It insures that those who enter the church will feel welcome and comfortable. It says to those who attend that the church cares for those who are within its fellowship.

This same concern is expressed in caring for the church building. The deacon leads the congregation in its stewardship over the facility, but this is an expression of care as well as of stewardship. He is concerned that the congregation is able to worship in an environment which is clean, orderly, and in good repair. The purpose is to care for the people who use the building as well as for the building itself.

Deacons are also called to minister in the homes of Saints. Their focus is in the area of service. They are to be especially conscious of physical or financial needs, and they should be more than willing to help when assistance is necessary. This kind of caring does not need to be limited to home ministry, however. Deacons may find that needs become apparent as they serve in an ushering capacity, or as they work with others in caring for the church facility, or in any other personal contacts which they have with the church.

In addition to the care which deacons provide directly, they can also teach the congregation about what it means to care and serve. In part, this is done by example. When they actively seek to recognize needs and move to meet them, deacons can show others what it means to offer a Christlike ministry of pastoral care. By maintaining an attitude of caring in some of the more mundane aspects of the office, they can provide new insights on what it means to act in a caring manner.

The deacon can also help others to find meaningful ways of offering service. This means he should be aware of the needs which exist in the congregation and the local community. Then, he can encourage persons within the church to offer service and ministry to meet those needs and to affirm the worth of those they encounter.

In a very real way, the ministry of the deacon bridges the separation which has been created between the sacred and secular. He understands the meaningful, spiritual nature of service which might sometimes appear to be unimportant.

Teacher

The teacher is called to understand the forces which unite people in the gospel as well as those forces which might separate persons from each other. Teachers are often called "peacemakers"; their unique ministry is most apparent when conflict arises and must be resolved. In practice, their ministry is much more extensive.

One of the reasons the office of teacher is so difficult to understand is that much of the work is not readily visible. When people gather for services, for example, a teacher may talk with them in the foyer before or after the service. He uses this time to discover opportunities and problems related to the relationships which the Saints have with each other and with those who are not members of the church.

If a teacher discovers that several persons are developing an interest in a particular hobby, for example, he might encourage them to share their ideas and progress with each other. They may even wish to work on a project in which they can use their hobby to benefit the church. Those interested in gardening, for example, may plant flowers and care for the shrubbery around the church. In this way, they can share with each other in a constructive manner which builds unity within the congregation. It also provides a constructive example to the congregation. The teacher may be the catalyst that brings these people together while not actually being a part of the group.

Informal visiting may also lead to the discovery of real or potential problems. To an astute teacher disagreements between individuals or divisions of opinion in a congregation may become apparent at a very early stage. When this happens, appropriate ministry may be offered which resolves the problem before it reaches a critical stage.

Similar types of ministry may also be rendered in the home or other less formal settings in which the teacher can work with individuals and families in a relatively relaxed and low-key manner. These types of ministry set the stage for those times when conflict becomes severe. If the teacher has a warm continuing relationship with the people involved, a dispute or conflict may be resolved much more effectively than it would be if he were not already known and trusted.

In addition to simply helping people solve problems, the teacher may encourage them to develop interpersonal skills which help to avoid or resolve conflict. Poor communication, for example, can result in conflicts when people misunderstand each other's motives and actions. The teacher can work constructively to prevent the occurrence of some conflicts.

Priest

A priest is called to develop and strengthen the ties that bind people together in the church and in families. That is, he is called to minister to persons in their relationships with each other. For example, he can perform some sacraments but not others. A close look at those in which he participates will indicate that they are the ones which build and strengthen relationships. Marriage, baptism by immersion, and the Communion either establish or strengthen ties that bind persons together in the church and the family. The priest's service as a family minister is an extension of that call.

While a strong sense of personal identity is important for everyone, it is also necessary for persons to see themselves as parts of groups. They do not live alone. Their lives are shared with others.

It is important, then, that priests spend time with

families in their homes, for this is where people make decisions about how they will live out the demands of the gospel. Today, family life in Western culture appears to be in some kind of transition. Many functions which formerly belonged to the family are now being provided by the larger community. This sometimes makes it appear that the importance of the family is declining. In fact, just the opposite is true. It is more important than ever that the family serve as a caring, loving, supportive community. Individual members of it must find ways of expressing the care, love, and support they are called to provide.

The task of the priest in this regard is difficult. Family relationships are very personal. While effective ministry must be given, it cannot be forced on people who do not want it. The priest, then, must struggle with the question of how to provide meaningful ministry without violating privacy. This requires his establishing ongoing relationships with families on the basis of trust. When he visits in a home, it might be appropriate for him to share suggestions for family worship, activities which might bring family members together, or other items which might be of interest.

Most important, however, the priest can bring an attitude of friendship and helpfulness so family members know that they can count on meaningful ministry when special needs or problems arise. Much of his ongoing ministry with a family will be centered on listening to the various members as they talk about the things that are important to them. By listening, he can show people that they are cared for and that their concerns are being heard.

Elder

The elder is called to lead individuals and groups to maturity. While men who serve in the Aaronic offices are concerned with providing the basic needs of persons and families, the elder is called to lead them to lives of increasing wholeness.

In other words, he is concerned with the long-term implications of the Christian life. Of course, many persons offer wise and mature ministry. The goal of the elder is to help more persons reach that point.

While he performs all of the sacraments and ordinances which are performed by the priest, an elder also participates in the ordinances of blessing children, administering to the sick, confirming new members and ordaining those called to the office of elder. These ordinances mark new possibilities for him. They symbolize God's continuing care and concern. They also require a significant degree of maturity on the part of the elder. He is called to understand life in its depth and breadth.

As one who offers pastoral care, the elder is particularly concerned with difficult problems of long standing and with possibilities which extend into the future. For example, he might very well develop skills in the area of counseling. In this way, he would be able to provide care in situations which call for particularly mature ministry, such as severe marital discord or personal problems.

On a more positive side, the elder may help persons and families to discover the possibilities for increasing richness and growth which might otherwise go unnoticed and unfulfilled. He may, for example, help persons or families develop potential gifts and talents which are present but of which they may be unaware.

On another level, the elder may serve in an administrative capacity. This indicates his call to recognize the possibilities for increasing growth and maturity which are present in the congregation as a whole. Many opportunities for ministry and fulfillment exist; he is called to discover them and help members of the congregation to see them.

The elder is a spiritual minister in the sense that spirituality represents a state of wholeness and completeness. Spirituality is the quality of life which brings depth, meaning, and cohesiveness to the experience of a person or group. Thus, the elder is to be a mature, stable, and insightful minister who offers consistently excellent pastoral care in the most difficult of situations.

DEVELOPING GIFTS AND TALENTS

Most priesthood calls represent a recognition of gifts and talents already present and capable of being developed. No one is ever ordained who already has the ability to perform all the duties of an office as well as they can possibly be performed. There is always a need for priesthood members to "magnify" their calling by developing the gifts and talents which they possess.

One important means of doing this is through regular prayer and meditation. This involves the ordained man looking at the world and himself "through the eyes of God." That is, he attempts to look openly and honestly at himself to find what his needs and strengths and weaknesses are. He also attempts to look compassionately at others in order to discover how he can be of service to them. Prayer and meditation are activities which should increase his ability to listen and observe, and they should help him to discover his strong points and limitations.

Another important way to develop gifts and talents is through study. As a priesthood member studies, he not only learns things that he needs to know but also begins to appreciate and respect those areas where his knowledge is lacking. In ministry, then, he can make use of those things which he knows and refer to others in areas where his understanding is limited.

There are several ways to study, and all of them have their place. The private reading of scriptures and other books is important; much can be learned in this way. It is also important to study with others so that ideas and insights can be tested in conversation and dialogue. This can be accomplished through local study groups, retreats, workshops, and courses offered by the Temple School in field schools and through home study.

Gifts and talents can also be developed by working with another person who is both knowledgeable and experienced in various areas of ministry. Much effective learning can result from watching someone do something well, talking together about it, and then trying it out under supervision.

All of these ways of developing gifts and talents can be helpful. The best learning occurs when all of them are used together so that insights learned in one way can be tried out in another context.

Closing Thoughts

Priesthood ministry is an important part of pastoral

care. It is a symbol of God's concern for humanity. It calls persons to develop special gifts and talents on behalf of others, and it provides a core group available to perform many of the tasks of pastoral care.

The call of priesthood to care is not exclusive, however. It represents and reminds all members of the larger call given to those who follow the Christ to act as agents of reconciliation and caring in his name. Many congregations have found it helpful to combine the ministry of priesthood with the ministry of others to provide pastoral care which makes use of the gifts and talents of the entire congregation.

Priesthood responsibility in pastoral care represents a call to serve. It is a call which gives a particular expression to the responsibility of all who would follow the Christ.

STUDY SUGGESTIONS

1. "Ministry, in its fullest sense, is the responsibility of the entire church."

    "The ministry of priesthood is a special function of this larger ministry of membership."

    What is your reaction to the way the author is defining ministry in general and the ministry of the priesthood?

2. "A call to a priesthood office is a call to service rather than a call to privilege." Do you agree? Why or why not?

3. The author describes several ways in which priesthood ministry is involved in pastoral care.

    a. Priesthood ministry is one indication that the

church desires to provide care on an intentional and systematic basis.
   b. Priesthood members are "caring" officers rather than "political" officers.
   c. Priesthood provides the church with the means to meet specific needs of individuals and families.
   Discuss the meaning and implication of each of these for congregational life.
4. "The authority of priesthood with regard to pastoral care is the authority to care and the authority to serve others in an exemplary way." What does the author mean by this statement? Do you agree? Why or why not?
5. The author shares how various priesthood offices relate to a pastoral care ministry. Summarize the points he made beside the following offices. After you do this, discuss the ways these caring activities are being lived out by the priesthood in your congregation.

Deacon:

Teacher:

Priest:

Elder:

6. The author states, "There is always a need for priesthood members to 'magnify' their calling by developing the gifts and talents which they possess." Discuss the value of this statement. The following ways of magnifying one's calling are shared:
   a. Regular prayer and meditation.
   b. Study.
   c. Working with a knowledgeable and experienced person.

   Discuss the advantages of each. Can you think of other ways that would help magnify one's calling?

PASTORAL CARE AND COUNSELING
by R. Daniel Fenn

At a reunion I recently attended I watched two people (I will call them Dick and Jane) relate to each other in a beautiful manner. Jane was a young woman who, because of physical disabilities, has felt different and, at times, very lonely. Dick was a young man who from all indications seemed to enjoy life. He smiled a lot and was friendly to everyone. I am sure that Jane believed she had very little to offer Dick. During a particular activity people were sitting in pairs and were supposed to share with each other their personal response to the statement, "If my grief were to speak it would say..." Quickly the sharing got very serious for each couple in the room. Every pair held their own special conversation. I could not hear what was being said by Jane and Dick, but the relationship was beautiful to observe. They shared intensely and, after a short while, Dick began to cry. Jane reached out to him and held him for a long time. She freely gave him pastoral care.

I talked with her briefly after this experience. She

said, "I always thought no one felt as lonely as I do, but I found out that Dick has similar feelings. He seemed so happy and cheerful I thought he had everything he wanted." Jane entered that relationship believing that she could only receive pastoral care and that she had nothing to offer in return. Instead, she discovered to her surprise that she had much to give. She listened to him, accepted his feelings, and held him. She exampled pastoral care at its best.

PASTORAL CARE
"Someone is standing on every person's road to God."

Pastoral care becomes a reality when persons are willing to be involved in helping relationships. This involvement seems a risk on the part of the helper and the helpee. Dick and Jane both risked. Dick shared his feelings with the risk that he could have been dismissed and laughed at by Jane. Jane reached out and held Dick with the risk that her help could have been rejected or misunderstood. Instead of these negative results Dick and Jane felt cared for, understood, accepted, worthwhile, and appreciated. We need to learn how to risk with each other in our church life.

If pastoral care is to come alive we also need to do away with the concept that "they" need pastoral care. Sometimes we describe "they" as people who are recently widowed, those involved in the process of divorce, children of broken homes, families struggling financially, or people with serious illnesses. No one would argue that pastoral care is needed in these situations, but it is time to become aware and admit the fact that "they" are "all" people—including you and me. Every person needs to feel cared for, worthy, accepted, and appreciated. We all need to express love and receive love in helping relationships. As long as we continue the false atmosphere of the "they" concept, we will continue having partial and limited pastoral care in our church life. Only when we are willing to let down our facades and risk, sharing with each other as Dick and Jane did, will pastoral care flourish in our churches.

The following quote will illustrate further what is meant by pastoral care.

> **Pastoral care is the communication of the gospel to persons at the point of their need. In II Corinthians 5:17-20 Paul writes that we are ambassadors for Christ, and to us is given the ministry and word of reconciliation that through us the world might be reconciled to God. As we live out our ambassadorship, people who come in contact with us will become new creatures; "old things are passed away and all things become new."**
>
> **We are called to communicate to people the good news of God's redeeming love as revealed in Jesus Christ. This is needed so that those who are lonely discover the meaning of community, those who have lost meaning find purpose again, those who are in despair find newness, those who are trapped in anxiety discover hope, those who are burdened with guilt experience forgiveness, and those who are caught in idolatry are freed to serve God in faith.[1]**

Jane was an ambassador of Christ in Dick's life. The "good news" of God's redeeming love was shared with him through her. All of us have this same calling—to give the ministry and word of reconciliation that through us the world might be reconciled to God. Young and old, men and women, priesthood and non-priesthood—all of us are ambassadors of the good news.

Pastoral care, then, is not something reserved for Sundays, not just a specific activity, but a life-style—a way of living our life in relation to other people and the broader world around us.

It makes all the difference in the world in what light we see life. You have heard it said that some people look at a glass of water and see it as half empty, whereas others see it as half full. Life can be seen, similarly—as half empty or half full. Seeing life as half empty means viewing it negatively and believing that the world is progressively getting worse, that people are out to take advantage of each other, and that there is little meaning to be found in existence. Seeing life as half full means viewing it positively and believing that the world is in the process of becoming whole, that people can be trusted and want to help each other, and that meaning is abundant. Those with the first view see earth as a place to endure; the second see it as a place to live. The first carry "bad news," whereas the second carry "good news."

At a recent reunion I helped with registrations. I watched as a young woman arrived and tentatively approached my table. She seemed very anxious and nervous. I tried to joke with her to help her relax, but it seemed to make matters worse. She never smiled and seemed ready to turn around and leave. The rest of the day she stayed mostly by herself and did not seem to have a good time. Two days later she approached me and said she wanted to talk. She expressed feelings of fear, loneliness, and worthlessness. She had been hurt deeply in the past by people who were close to her, and she didn't want to feel that pain again. She did not want to be at the reunion but felt forced to attend by her family. After she had talked for about an hour I began to feel a real friendship for her. I accepted her feelings as real and important, but I also confronted her. I sensed her need to relate meaningfully with others, but her fears were blocking this from happening. I shared with her the fact that there were many at this particular reunion who also had been hurt in previous relationships and could identify with her pain. I also shared my belief that those same people were willing to accept her and share meaningfully with her if she gave them a chance. As we ended our conversation I was still not sure what her choice would be. That night there was a reunion roller-skating party. I entered the room, got my skates, and began putting them on. All of a sudden a smiling, cheerful woman came skating up to me and said, "Can you tell a difference?" I said, "I certainly can. I guess you've decided to have a good time." She was a different person the rest of the week. Earlier, because of her feelings of fear and worthlessness, she needed a lot of pastoral care, but she had very little to give. Now, because of a change in her attitude, she was able to both give and receive pastoral care. Her half empty glass was becoming half full. She had decided to live instead of just endure. She was beginning to cultivate a pastoral care life-style.

Such a life-style emanates good news. It means

accepting people no matter what their past has been or what their present is. It means respecting their feelings and treating them as worthwhile children of God. It means trying to understand the feelings of others and to be with them in their pain and struggle. It means seeing life realistically with all its ups and downs, yet always holding up to people the hope in life's possibilities. It means cultivating the ability to sense a sanctity of life where common happenings have new and profound meaning, and relationships between people are opportunities for receiving and giving the good news. It means being willing to risk oneself *for* another person and/or being willing to risk oneself *to* another person.

It has been my experience that the statement, "Someone is standing on every person's road to God" is true. As we search for the ultimate in life (God), we continually come in contact with significant persons who influence us. We need to realize both our calling to share God's good news with those whose road we are standing on and our calling to risk and allow others to share God's good news with us when we come upon people on our road to God.

Viewing pastoral care in this light means that every individual has opportunities each day to be involved in helping relationships. In every encounter with another human being there is the possibility of growth and meaning. In a helping relationship both the helper and the helpee can grow and find meaning.

COUNSELING

"The counselor's task is... to heal sometimes, to remedy often, to comfort always."[2]

Counseling is one form of pastoral care. It involves a relationship between a person who has some training and a client. Perhaps I should clarify what is meant by a "counseling relationship" as compared to a "helping relationship" that most of us are involved in every day.

> **Counseling covers all types of two-person situations in which one person, the client, is helped to adjust more effectively to himself (herself) and to his (her) environment.—Robinson**
>
> **Counseling is a talking over, a conference, a friendly discussion, upon equal terms, with no attempt to impose decision, and with every effort to stimulate the thought of the student to find or generate such technical knowledge and wisdom as will lead him (her) to a right decision.—Brewer**

Counseling occurs in a relationship between a client, who is helped in some way, and a counselor, who provides the client with an environment for growth and decision making. The counselor is preferably someone who has had training and is either a professional or a paraprofessional (lay counselor).

Counseling and helping relationships do have some things in common. Before counseling can be successful—no matter what model or techniques are used—an atmosphere conducive to change and growth should exist. This includes empathy, respect, and genuineness. (These conditions were not directly discussed in the previous section on pastoral care, but if you reread the examples of helping relationships given you will discover their presence.) If these conditions exist in a relationship, there is a possibility of growth and change occurring. Both a healthy helping relationship and a meaningful counseling relationship have these conditions present.

Empathy is the ability of the counselor to feel with the client. Even though it is impossible to totally "feel" the same as another person, the counselor tries to come as close as possible. It is not enough just to understand the feelings of a client, however; a counselor also needs to be able to communicate this understanding, both verbally and nonverbally. When this occurs the client can relate to the one who is listening and will feel more inclined to "open up." Such opening up occurs at different time intervals with various clients. I can remember some who came into my office and, after I made only a couple of empathic responses, proceeded to "tell it all." Others, however, needed many sessions and a great deal of empathic responses before they were willing to finally risk sharing their real concerns.

It is important to understand that empathy is different from sympathy. Empathy is feeling *with* someone, whereas sympathy is feeling *for* the person. Empathy implies involvement in the feelings of the client, whereas sympathy implies feeling sorry for the client but not necessarily being involved in his/her feelings.

Respect is the ability of the counselor to accept the client as a person of worth. This has its origin in the counselor's own self-respect—a prerequisite for respecting others. The counselor does not need to condone the client's behavior, which can be separated from that person's worth as an important human being. When respect exists two things happen. First, clients feel free to express their concerns because they know they will not be rejected; second, they begin to have more self-respect and eventually their behavior will reveal this newly found self-respect.

I once counseled a woman who had lost all respect for herself because of the life-style she had adopted. She believed she deserved all the guilt and agony she was experiencing. Since she felt she did not deserve anything better, she just continued being involved in the self-defeating behaviors which were destroying her. She was caught in a vicious cycle. She would not share her concern with others because she knew they would reject her... so she carried her hurt all alone. Finally, she found herself in a loving environment, and she risked sharing who she was with me. I accepted her and listened to her. I seemed to understand her pain. I did not condemn or reject her. I tried to help her accept herself and accept what she really wanted for herself. I respected her as a child of God. By my accepting her—even though I knew about her behavior—she gradually began to regain her self-respect and started making different decisions concerning her behavior. Her self-defeating cycle, leading to more and more feelings of worthlessness, became a growth-producing cycle, leading to more and more feelings of respect and worth.

Genuineness is the ability of counselors to be honest with themselves and, in turn, with their clients. A genuine relationship between the two is extremely important. Honesty on the part of the counselor breeds honesty on the part of the client. This process does two things. First, it helps clients disclose concerns they need to express and talk over; second, it helps clients be honest with themselves in ways that facilitate growth and change.

At the beginning of this chapter I mentioned talking with a woman at reunion. Her fears were blocking her from relating meaningfully with others. Realizing this might be my only opportunity to confront her with herself, I decided to be as honest as I could with her, hoping that I would come across in an empathic and respectful way. So I told her how I was perceiving her fears, what I believed she was really wanting, and challenged her not to turn away from this opportunity to experience a loving community. My honesty with her allowed her to be honest with herself. She proceeded to face who she was and who she wanted to be that week, and the change which took place in her was beautiful to watch.

Once again, these atmospheric conditions are important to both a helping relationship and a counseling relationship. Counseling and pastoral care, then, share the same basic qualities as a *starting point* for helping others, but counseling also includes much more. In the rest of this section I shall write about the *more*.

If counselors are "to heal sometimes, to remedy often, to comfort always," they need to have special training in order to accomplish these goals with clients. Just as medical doctors learn certain procedures and use various medicines to cure their patients, so counselors develop a personal style, using various theories and techniques in order to help their clients.

As I stated earlier, a counseling relationship is different from the helping relationships in which most of us are involved every day. A counseling relationship is more structured and formal than the typical informal helping relationship. For instance, in counseling a client usually comes to the counselor's office for a specified amount of time, between thirty and sixty minutes depending on such factors as the age and functioning level of the client. A counseling relationship occurs over a specified number of sessions depending on the seriousness of the concern and the progress of the client.

The focus of the counseling relationship is on the client, not the counselor. Client needs determine the goals and direction of the counseling. The techniques and strategies the counselor chooses to use are for the sole purpose of helping clients deal with their concerns. Everything they say is respected by the counselor as being confidential. Confidentiality is defined differently by various counselors, but a definition I appreciate is that the counselor will treat everything said by the client with respect and will share only segments of conversation for the good of the client. It is clear from this definition the enormous trust a client must have in any counselor chosen.

The counseling relationship, basically, goes through three phases—early, middle, and final.

The early phase covers the process of the counselor and client making contact. This is the time during which the atmospheric conditions of empathy, respect, and genuineness are established. Together the counselor and client begin exploring the client's concerns. In the early phase roles are established, and counseling goals and expectations are clarified. The counselor and client become comfortable with each other and prepare to get down to work.

COUNSELING PHASES

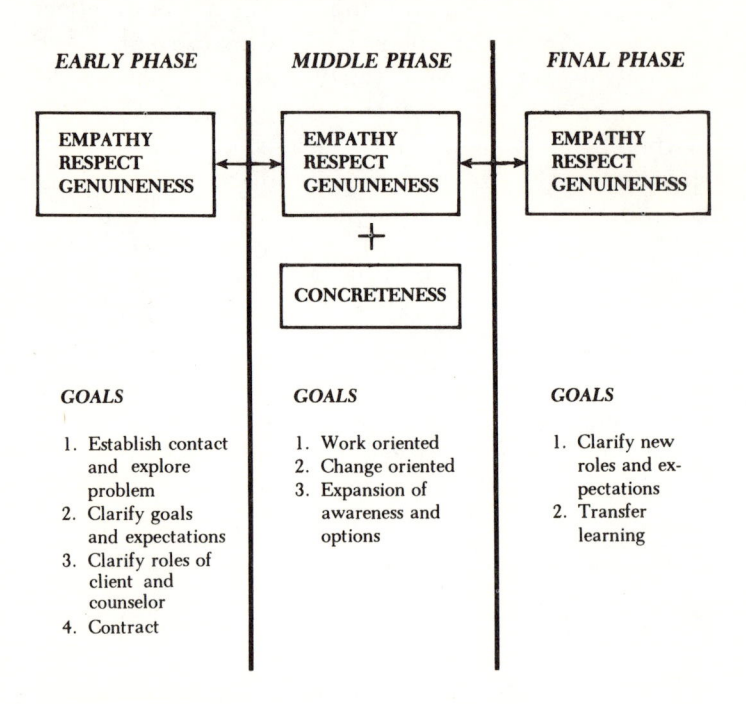

EARLY PHASE	MIDDLE PHASE	FINAL PHASE
EMPATHY RESPECT GENUINENESS	EMPATHY RESPECT GENUINENESS + CONCRETENESS	EMPATHY RESPECT GENUINENESS
GOALS 1. Establish contact and explore problem 2. Clarify goals and expectations 3. Clarify roles of client and counselor 4. Contract	*GOALS* 1. Work oriented 2. Change oriented 3. Expansion of awareness and options	*GOALS* 1. Clarify new roles and expectations 2. Transfer learning

During this early phase is the time the counseling and helping relationships are somewhat similar in that they are centered on caring for and supporting a person who is in need. The middle and final phases of counseling more clearly distinguish the differences.

The middle "working phase" of counseling is when therapeutic change should begin to occur in the life of the client. The atmospheric conditions are still present, but the counselor and client now become more specific and intentional in their work. The particular methods or techniques counselors use will depend on how they view change occurring in people's lives. For example, some counselors believe people change when they have new insight into their concerns, whereas other counselors believe change occurs when people are reinforced to behave differently. The way counselors perceive change greatly influences how they proceed.

In the middle phase the counselor and client work on the goals that were established in the early phase. Sometimes these will change, but it is important for both persons to keep goals in view.

This phase is also a time to expand the client's awareness and explore all the options available. For example, a young high school girl discovers she is pregnant and decides to discuss her problem with the school counselor. After a relationship is established (early phase) they begin exploring options. One of the goals is for her to have as much information as possible before she decides what would be best for her to do. Appointments are made at a child adoption agency and planned parenthood (abortion counseling) so she can learn more about these possibilities. With the counselor she explores other options, such as keeping the baby and remaining single, getting married, and having the baby and allowing a relative to rear the child while she finishes school. After exploring all these options she has a better chance to make a decision with which she can live.

In the final phase counseling comes to an end. The atmospheric conditions are present as always, but now the counselor and client clarify changes and "learnings." When the client is ready to face life and make decisions without the counselor, counseling is terminated. It is hoped that when new concerns arise, the client will be able to deal effectively with them because of the counseling experience.

It is extremely important to remember that all these phases occur under the umbrella of the atmospheric conditions. Without them it is difficult to accomplish anything; with them—and with a trained counselor and willing client—a meaningful and growth-producing relationship can develop.

If you are interested in becoming a trained counselor you may want to check the educational institutions in your area for information on the programs they offer. Another option would be to check into paraprofessional training programs near you. Sometimes persons are trained in short-term community programs for crisis telephone work or other types of community service. A paraprofessional program that the Reorganized Church of Jesus Christ of Latter Day Saints offers would be another option. It is called the Lay Counseling Program.

LAY COUNSELING PROGRAM

> Many psychologists and psychotherapists will be horrified at the conclusion that psychotherapy is not a profession but something that can be taught to many persons, persons who lack a college education or a background in psychology. Yet this is the logical extension of the recognition that the essence of psychotherapy is that it is a good human relationship.[4]

Almost every member of the church at one time or another could benefit from talking with a person who has counseling training. Crises such as death, serious illness, financial problems, and divorce are no respecter of persons or families. The church is full of caring and loving individuals who try to help during these hard times, but sometimes the people affected are left lonely, depressed, and/or hurt. This is when it would be helpful to have lay counselors available. Members could receive competent help from other members whom they trust and with whom they feel comfortable.

The Lay Counseling Program is not a substitute or replacement of priesthood and member responsibility to people in need. Rather, it is an important supplemental ministry. Many times in the life of the church we can testify of situations where priesthood and members in general said or did just the right thing to help someone who was troubled. The problem, however, is that there also are situations where persons with the best intentions said or did the wrong thing which made matters worse for the person needing help. All of us need to know our limitations. Even though I am a trained counselor, I recognize there will be times when I will need to refer clients to someone else so they can receive adequate help. Priesthood and members can use the lay counselors in their jurisdictional area as such a referral group. The Lay Counseling Program can provide a meaningful and vitally needed supplemental ministry in the life of the church.

The program was initiated as a pilot project in the spring of 1975. Since its inception it has grown and developed. The philosophy behind Patterson's statement on psychotherapy given at the beginning of this section is the basis of the program. It has been found through research that persons who possess warmth and ego-strength (believe in themselves) make successful lay counselors if given sufficient training and guidance from a professional counselor. A brief description of the program will help explain how we have fit this theory into actual practice.

The administrator of a district, stake, or region can request a lay counseling workshop. The administrator in the area also selects a degreed counselor to supervise the program. Persons are then selected to be trained as lay counselors. This selection originates mainly through recommendations by the administrator and degreed counselor and through persons volunteering to be involved. As soon as the degreed counselor and lay counselors are chosen, a staff person from the Pastoral Care Office holds a weekend workshop with them. This covers a variety of subjects, such as a model for counseling, crisis counseling, and referral counseling. Plenty of time is allotted for role playing so the lay counselors can begin practicing what they learn. After this initial workshop the lay counseling group is supervised totally by the degreed counselor. This person is in charge of coordinating further training events and meetings for the group, of directing public relations for group members so they will be known around the jurisdictional area, and of supervising the counseling relationships of each lay counselor.

The success of a lay counseling group depends on at least two things. First, the total support of the administrator and leaders in that area is needed. This is vital for the acceptance of the lay counselors by pastors, priesthood, and members so referrals will be made to the group. Second, the program demands so much from the degreed counselor and lay counselors that they need to be totally committed to it. If both of these are present, there is a high possibility for success.

The Lay Counseling Program has much to offer the church. The groups already in existence have helped many individuals and families in the church and those who are friends of the church. If there is a group already organized in your area you may wish to get better acquainted with and possibly use it as a referral in your ministry with others. If a group has not been started in your area, perhaps plans can be made to move in this way.

CONCLUDING THOUGHTS

It is in living a pastoral care life-style that we emanate the "good news"; that life has meaning and that our lives have purpose; that God loves every one and that we are called to share that love with each other; that in Christ we can become new creatures. Jane and Dick shared pastoral care with each other. They experienced the "good news" of the gospel as they risked caring for each other. They found meaning, felt the love of God, and became new creatures. We are called to do likewise.

Empathy, respect, and genuineness are the underlying factors which create healthy helping relationships and successful counseling relationships. All of us need to develop these qualities in our personal lives. As we risk in caring and sharing with these qualities in our relationships, we will grow as God's people.

REFERENCES
1. Daniel R. Fenn, "To Care with Love," *Commission* magazine, September, 1976.
2. Wayne E. Oates, *Pastoral Counseling* (Philadelphia: Westminster Press), 1974.
3. Robert R. Carkhuff and Bernard G. Berenson, *Beyond Counseling and Therapy* (New York: Holt, Rinehart and Winston, Inc.), 1967.
4. C. H. Patterson, *Relationship Counseling and Psychotherapy* (New York: Harper & Row, Publishers), 1974.

STUDY SUGGESTIONS

1. The author shares the need to do away with the concept that "they" need pastoral care. All people, including you, need pastoral care. If this is true, what are your pastoral care needs? Share these with each other.
2. The author mentions a variety of elements which would help an individual and a congregation live a pastoral care life-style. These elements are as follows:
   a. Persons need to be willing to be involved in helping relationships.
   b. Persons need to be willing to let down their facades and accept their need to give and receive pastoral care.
   c. Every person ought to recognize the calling to give pastoral care ministry.
   d. Individuals and congregations should realize the need to develop a pastoral care life-style.
   e. People need to see life as positive, to see the world in the process of becoming whole, to believe that people can be trusted and want to help each other,

and that meaning is abundant in life.
Discuss each of these elements. What implications do they have for individuals and for the congregation?
3. What has been your experience concerning the quote: "Someone is standing on every person's road to God"? If it has been true for you, who has been standing on your road to God?
4. Discuss the meaning and implications of the atmospheric conditions (empathy, genuineness, and respect) for both the counseling relationship and helping relationship. Are these three conditions important to you in your relationships? If so, in what ways?
5. Does your jurisdictional area have a Lay Counseling Group? If so, how can you benefit from it? (If not, you may want to talk to your jurisdictional officers about establishing one.)

PASTORAL CARE ACTIVITIES
by Carol Anderson Anway

Is pastoral care just another fad which will generate enthusiasm for a while and then pass into oblivion? We would certainly hope not. The caring-for-others principle which it conceptualizes is basic to the living out of our Christian beliefs.

Pastoral care takes place in relationships between people. Often this experience occurs spontaneously as caring persons interact with others, but it can most consistently and effectively occur in structured, planned activities between two individuals, in small groups, in large gatherings, in fun times, or in serious times such as corporate worship. Common settings in which pastoral care may occur are church family nights, church school picnics, potluck meals, weddings, funerals, and seasonal celebrations. At these times activities for group interaction may be planned and facilitated.

As you have read various articles in this book, your mind probably has begun to overflow with ideas relative to your particular situation. You may have considered how you might help create situations and settings in which nurturing and affirming may take place in your church group. Each community and congregation is unique and different. Yet the common denominator is apparent in the need of all persons to be loved, accepted, and supported, as well as to know and love and accept others of varying ages. It is through knowing and caring activities that pastoral care can take place. The following activities are suggestions that may assist you in providing opportunities for people to experience this kind of knowing, caring, and communicating.

SMALL GROUP ACTIVITIES

Included here are many small group activities which can be used at various settings in your branch or congregation. These have the purpose of helping people to get to know each other in greater depth. Often we know one another's names but little about our lives. By trying to express ourselves and something about our lives in these small groups, we learn more about who we are. Some very interesting facts emerge in regard to our own thoughts. These activities might be used at a family night where those present are divided into small groups. Each activity provides ways to facilitate communication and caring. The activities may be used by youth, priesthood, women, and intergenerational groups.

COMMUNICATION AND CARING ACTIVITIES

1. AN INVENTORY OF ME
Goal: To help participants to become better ac-

quainted with each other and to find out about themselves.

Time: The major activity takes about ten minutes. Sharing time depends on the number of persons present and how many share.

Age: Eight years through adult.

Materials: Sheet of paper and pencil or felt-tipped pen for each person present.

Procedure

a. Invite all in the group to draw a circle in the center of their sheets of paper, and write their names in the circle.

b. Have them draw four circles—one at the top of the paper, one at the bottom, and one on each side. Connect to the center circle with lines. In the top circle they

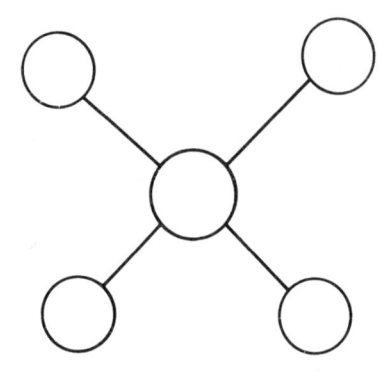

—Adapted from *Developing the Art of Discussion*, Judson Press, 1977. The authors are indebted to Dr. Rich Hause, professor of Curriculum and Instruction, Kansas State University, for the idea of this activity. Used by permission of Judson Press.

are to write three books they have recently read. In the next circle (going to the right) write three things they hate to do but must do. In the next circle, write three things they do well. And in the last circle, write three things they want to learn to do.

These papers may be shared in small groups or displayed around the room for sharing in larger groups.

2. **GETTING TO KNOW YOU**
   Goal: To get to know each other on an in-depth basis in groups of two.
   Time: Thirty to forty-five minutes.
   Age: Eight years through adult.
   Preparation of Materials: Provide a set of "Getting to Know You" cards for each pair, have the questions listed (with a number before each question) on a large sheet of paper which everyone can see. Provide cards with the numbers one through ten or eleven (depending on the number of questions) so participants may draw a number and ask the question that matches that number.

   Possible Questions for the Cards:

   - If you were president of the church now, what would be your first directive?
   - What is the most pressing problem facing our church today?

- What do you like most about our congregation or branch?
- If you could choose your own name, what would it be?
- On a rainy day, would you rather listen to music, read, sleep, or walk in the rain?
- What is your favorite time of the year?
- What is your favorite scripture story? Why?
- Name a place you would like to visit. Tell why.
- What do you consider your major strength? Tell why.
- What do you consider your major weakness? Tell why.
- What do you like best about your church school class?

Create similar questions of your own to fit your specific situation.

Procedure

a. Divide the persons present into pairs.
b. Provide each pair with either a set of "Getting to Know You" cards or a set of numbers corresponding to the large questions on display. The persons in each pair take turns drawing either one card or one number at a time and asking the information of each other. Allow 15-20 minutes for this.

    c. These persons may then use the information they have gathered to introduce their partners in the large group gathering. If the whole group is small (not over fifteen persons) meet together for the sharing of introductions by partners. If large, divide into groups of eight to twelve.

—Adapted from *Developing the Art of Discussion*, Judson Press, 1977. Used by permission of Judson Press.

3. *I LIKE PEOPLE WHO...*

Goal: To establish trust by sharing personally with those around you.

Time: Fifty minutes.

Age: Eight years through adult.

Materials: Pencil and mimeographed sheets of paper containing the following statements:

I like people who...

In my spare time I love to...

The best thing about school or my work is...

I am irritated when...

I wish my parents/children wouldn't...

I feel best when I'm with a group of people who...

I feel bad when I'm with a group of people who...

When I'm around adults/small children I feel...

Strangers make me feel...

When I'm 20/30/60/80 I think I'll be...
When there is no right answer, I feel...
Other people regard me as ....

Procedure
- a. Ask each person to complete the page of sentences. Ten minutes should be allowed for this part.
- b. Divide the main group into smaller groups of four or five. Try to have a variety of ages represented in each group if families are participating. Share responses to each of these questions on a voluntary basis, dealing with one question at a time. At the end of thirty minutes someone should call time.
- c. Share in the large group gathering any special insights that came from the writing and sharing.

—Adapted from *Developing the Art of Discussion*, Judson Press, 1977. Used by permission of Judson Press.

4. MAKING A "Me"
Goal: To establish trust by working with another partner in sharing about one's self and working together on a project.
Time: Forty minutes.
Age: Four years through adult.
Materials: Six feet (or more) of white or brown wrapping paper or newsprint for each person, large felt pens, crayons, and scissors.

Display on large paper the statements to be written on various parts of the drawn figures.

Procedure
- a. Work in pairs; if there are children in the group they probably should work with an adult. Give each couple two sheets of paper and felt pen. Have crayons and scissors available.
- b. One of the pair lies on the paper while the partner draws around the person. After the outline is complete, the person gets off the paper and completes the statements on various parts of the body.
- c. The other partner is then drawn. Both work on their statements together, discussing as they respond. Or one person's figure and statements may be completed before attempting the partner's.
- d. If there is time, cut out the figures, turn them over and draw in the features and clothing.
- e. When finished, share the portraits. They may be hung around the room with masking tape while they are being shared. Felt-tip pens may be used to decorate, but be careful not to obscure the writing.

Something I would like to learn

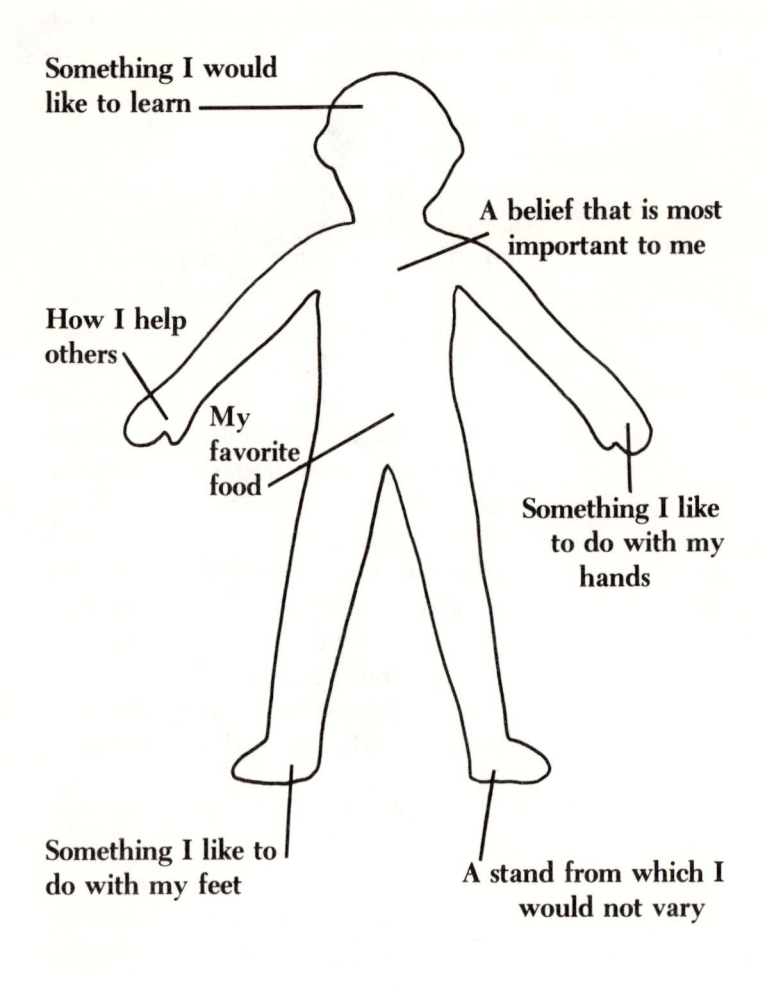

A belief that is most important to me

How I help others

My favorite food

Something I like to do with my hands

Something I like to do with my feet

A stand from which I would not vary

—Adapted from *Developing the Art of Discussion*, Judson Press, 1977. Used by permission of Judson Press.

5. BANNERS

Goal: To have fun making a banner about one's self and sharing this banner with others in a trusting environment.

Time: Thirty-five minutes.

Age: Four years through adult. (The younger ones may need some help.)

Materials: Four-inch-wide strips of newsprint or butcher paper at least two yards in length (one per person), magazines, crayons, glue, scissors, and masking tape.

Procedure

a. Distribute one of the long banners to each person. Place magazines, crayons, glue, and scissors in a convenient location.

b. Participants may fold their banners in half, decorating only one side. Have them cut from magazines any pictures, headlines, phrases, or words that they feel describe how others see them, and glue these to the banner. They may also draw on the banner words or symbols describing how they think others see them.

c. Have participants unfold their banners and place the fold on the right shoulder, drawing the decorated part of the banner across the chest and over to the left side. The undecorated part goes over the back and to the left side.

d. Ask them to circulate around the room

and share with each other how they feel others see them. Encourage them not to spend more than one minute per person. A timer may be used to keep the movement going.

6. **AUTOBIOGRAPHICAL PICTURES**

   Goal: To establish communication with other persons about my life.

   Time: Forty-five minutes.

   Age: Eight years through adult.

   Materials: Pencils, paper for each person; fine felt-pens may be used rather than pencils.

   Procedure

   a. Ask the persons to write a simple autobiography on their paper using only symbols or pictures, no words. It should be organized and clear enough that someone else could read it and learn something about the person. Allow ten minutes for the drawing.

   b. Divide into groups of six to eight persons. Ask each group to form a circle.

   c. Ask students to exchange papers with another person and then have that person "read" the other's autobiography showing the symbols used to the rest of the group. The author should be given some time to respond to the interpretation of his/her story. Try to spend no more than five minutes per person.

   —Adapted from *Developing the Art of Discussion*, Judson Press, 1977. Used by permission of Judson Press.

7. SHARING SELF AND REFRESHMENTS

Goal: To use the refreshment period as a special time of sharing in small groups.

Time: Thirty minutes.

Age and Setting: For any group with persons eight to ten and older. May be used any time at a meeting where refreshments are served (e.g., women's meeting, family night, or senior adult meeting).

Materials: Card tables (enough for participants to be divided into small groups of four or five to each table) and candles. Refreshments (e.g., relish plate, dip, and fruit juice).

Preparation
  a. Set up tables and decorate with candles, flowers, etc.
  b. Number each table.
  c. Ask one person who knows everyone well to assign the group to tables (or those present may count off or just go to the tables of their choice).
  d. Decide on topics for group response and print them on index cards, one card for each table leader. Topics might be as follows:
   - Tell about when you first remember being in church.
   - Tell about a time you really felt close to God.
   - Tell what most concerns you right now in life.

- Take turns praying either aloud or silently about the concerns of the person on your left until each at the table has been remembered in prayer.

e. Ahead of time arrange for a person at each table to lead the group in responding to the questions on the index card. Ask one or two persons to serve refreshments for the whole group. *Note:* It is effective to have the part of the meeting prior to refreshments in another part of the building. Light the candles before the participants come in. Part or all of the refreshments may already be on the table.

Procedure

a. Give instructions about the refreshments and seating before going to the refreshment area.
b. Have participants seated at tables in the refreshment area.
c. Have group leaders read the first topic to their groups and invite each member to share his/her answers. Then continue on through the list, sharing on each topic.
d. Suggest that serving begin immediately if food isn't already on the tables. (Leaders should encourage group members to eat while listening to others share.)
e. Give the groups a five-minute warning

before time to close.
   f. Close with an all-group song such as "Blest Be the Tie That Binds" and/or scripture or prayer of benediction.

8. *WHEN A FAMILY IS LEAVING*
   Goal: To help members of a family who are moving (or persons leaving for college or the armed services) feel appreciated and affirmed.
   Time: Ten minutes.
   Age: All ages.
   Setting: Worship setting such as the Sunday morning service or family night devotional.
   Preparation: Arrange with the family to be present. Plan the service to end with the following:

Procedure
   a. In the service
      Leader: "We have with us the_____ family [name them one by one and call them forward]. This is their last [or one of the last] time(s) to meet with us. [Then suggest ways they have contributed to the group.] They will be in the reception line as you leave this service so that each of you may personally express your regards to them."
      To the family:
         The Lord bless and keep you.
         The Lord make his face to shine

upon you and be gracious
unto you.

The Lord lift up his countenance
upon you and give you peace.

Congregation: "God Be with You Till
We Meet Again"
Prayer (for the family or one leaving)
Response: Doxology

b. Invite the family or individual to stand in the reception line to be greeted by the people as they leave.

9. *IMPORTANT LIFE POINTS*

Goal: To assist persons in learning about themselves through choosing important points in their development.

To help them share this self-awareness with others.

Time: Sixty minutes.

Age: Adult.

Materials: Four small slips of paper and a pencil for each person.

Procedure

a. Hand out a pencil and four slips of paper to everyone present. Ask those participating to think back to their childhood and decide on an important moment they remember in their development. Have them write a word or phrase on a slip of paper to help them recall it.

b. Next, ask them to think of their teen

years and choose one memory of those years they feel was an important point in their development. Write a word or phrase on another slip of paper to help them recall it.
c. Do this for the young adult years.
d. Ask participants to think of the most recent event that has been important in their personal development.
e. Ask the participants, in groups of four to six, to share these significant times, beginning with the childhood experience. After everyone shares on the first, continue to the important moments from the teens, young adult years, and the most recent experience. Ask that each one in the group share on one level before going to the next.
f. Closing: Ask each person to summarize the personal discovery made in this sharing. This may be done in the large group.

10. VISITING

Goal: To visit each family in the congregation.
To deliver the congregational/branch yearbook.

Setting: Many congregations develop a congregational/branch yearbook, including information regarding
a. Local and district/stake officers.
b. Membership by families (with phone

numbers and addresses).
  c. General month-by-month plans of various groups, such as women's meetings, church officers meetings, young adult plans, senior adult group meetings, family night dates, themes, and emphases.
  d. Traditional meetings such as priesthood visiting and Cub Scout meetings.
  e. Visiting may be organized by using priesthood, women, couples, or even families.

Time: Fifteen to thirty minutes per visit, plus transportation.

Preparation
  a. Organize and prepare information for yearbook; print and assemble.
  b. Determine method of visiting and distribution.
  c. Recruit visitors.

Procedure for visitors
  a. Call ahead to arrange a visit with the family for fifteen minutes to one-half hour, indicating why you're coming.
  b. On arrival, be friendly; go over the yearbook briefly with the family.
  c. Visit briefly. Close with prayer if it seems appropriate.

11. *GUESS WHO'S COMING TO DINNER*
  Goal: To encourage visiting and togetherness among members of the congregation.

Time: Two hours or more following church on Sunday morning.

Age: All ages.

Procedure

    a. For several weeks prior to the event, announce in various ways the following: "On Sunday ____[date]____, we are going to have a *Guess Who's Coming to Dinner*. We need two groups of volunteers. One group of volunteers are to be those who will offer to be the hosts in their homes to feed those from the other group of volunteers. This other group of volunteers are the ones who will be the dinner guests. We will do this again in a few weeks so the ones who cook this time can volunteer to be guests next time, and guests this time can volunteer to provide the dinner. Please consult in your families before you volunteer so your family is involved in the decision."

    b. Provide lists on the bulletin board or have someone designated to accept names. You may need to do some recruiting for volunteers in both groups.

    c. Assign guest families to host families, but keep the list secret. By Thursday evening let the host family know how many to expect (but do not reveal the names).

    d. After church Sunday send the hosts on

home. Then give the guest families each a slip of paper with the name of their hosts and directions to the home of their hosts. Be sure to arrange for anyone needing transportation.
e. At the next Sunday morning service arrange a time when both guests and hosts have opportunity to share about the dinner and visit.
f. Important: Plan another visit in a few weeks.

Over the years there have been many activities suggested in the annual issue of the *Congregational Leaders Handbook* that would enrich the caring and communication of pastoral units. Several of these activities are reprinted in the following pages under the headings: "Creative Sharing Activities," "Special Times," "Worship," "Weekend Events," and "Audio-Visual Resources."

CREATIVE SHARING ACTIVITIES

These activities may be used in many settings, but they basically provide ideas to facilitate communication of feelings, ideas, and experiences among participants. These may be adapted to your own unique setting for a variety of meetings or groups.
  a. *Caring for Others:* Have a reflection session in your church at which people explore how well the people are caring for one another. Include a variety of people for providing input—a senior citizen,

youth, single person, divorced person, widow or widower, young parents, etc. Reaffirm all the ways you are presently caring for one another, and make plans for caring more effectively in those areas where people feel that care is lacking.

b. *Interview Testimonies:* Interview three or four older persons in the church about their testimonies of God's love. This may be done during a special service, family night, or prechurch-school worship. They will feel more secure if you let them know ahead of time what questions you plan to ask.

c. *Sharing About a Meaningful Book:* Plan a "Books That Change Lives" sharing time when persons of all ages bring one of their favorite books. Ask each to be prepared to briefly tell the main significant concept(s).

d. *Sharing Skills—"Awareness of Us":* One way to learn about one's self and others in the congregation is to set up times when people's skills can be shared. A series of Sunday nights could be set aside for this purpose. The theme, "Awareness of Us," could lead the planning. Members could share through music, written material, photography, art, drama, humor, baked goods, crafts, storytelling, etc.

e. *Giving Persons Positive Regard:* Arrange chairs in a circle or horseshoe with an empty one apart from the others. Ask each individual to sit one at a time in the chair while the entire group bombards the individual with positive terms regarding how they feel about him/her. People may speak whenever they think of something, or each may add something in turn—such as "honesty," "frugality," and "sincerity." Help the group understand that the objective is to build up the person. No negative comments of any kind should be allowed. If many are present, divide into groups of four to eight persons.

f. ***Getting to Know Each Other:*** As persons arrive for the evening, pair individuals with someone they do not know well. Ask each to interview the other for five to seven minutes, finding out everything possible about the individual—favorite foods, hobbies, television shows, family facts, educational plans, and the like. All persons should interview their partners simultaneously. After the time limit has been reached, arrange participants into groups of six to ten persons and ask each one to introduce his or her friend in depth to the entire group. Perhaps the introducer will want to ask other group members to add little known facts. Alternatives or additional activities might include sharing three things each individual would save from his or her home if only three things could be saved.

g. ***Sharing Review of Summer Activities:*** Most people remember and will enthusiastically share accounts of previous summer activities. As a way to prepare for this year's activities, plan a program which encourages sharing. Families and/or individuals might bring slides, home movies, or oral reports of "what we did last summer—or last vacation" emphasizing such things as (1) how we felt about the chance for recreation—a change of pace; (2) interesting people we met and/or experiences we had; (3) what we would do differently if we had time and money available again. Ask the same individuals or family groups to share plans for the next summer or next vacation. Emphasize creativity, support of the church during travel, making offerings to the home congregation before leaving on vacation, etc.

- *h. Brainstorming About Local Resources:* Have a symposium. Invite about four or five persons (variety of ages and sexes) to sit around a table for a conversation about the following: What gifts and talents are most needed in the local church? What gifts are already present? If we had these gifts, what could we do differently? What resources are available to help people grow personally so their gifts and talents are enlarged and enhanced? After a time the facilitator may invite observers to enter into the discussion so the whole congregation can talk together about its needs.
- *i. We Remember Supportive Times:* Only in a supportive atmosphere can persons develop wholistically. Members of the church are encouraged to give support to each other. Together plan an experience in which members relate what someone else has done or said which made them feel good about themselves. Suggest that families may occasionally repeat this activity in their homes.
- *j. We Pray for Each Other:* It is always nice to know that people are praying for one another. Set up a prayer system within the church so that everyone

is included. Change the persons for whom each member is praying occasionally. Wherever members travel, whatever problems they might have, they will know that someone is praying for them. This can be a great source of strength.

k. ***Concern for Others in the Faith:*** Attempt to motivate disinterested members by having a church family "adopt" them, on the basis of love and need for them as persons—involving them in shared family activities and church-related fellowship.

l. ***Establish Support Groups:*** The lives of people are continually changing. As much as we would like for things to stay constant, this is not the way life is lived. People are born, leave home, become seriously ill, and die; relationships are broken. All of us need support and love during times of crisis in our lives. We need to be assured of the love of God. Congregations could help people facing these crises by organizing grief groups, single groups, divorce groups, or couple groups. Persons in the community could also be invited to join a group.

SPECIAL TIMES

There are times to celebrate in the church. These are just three examples of how the celebration might take place.

a. ***For Easter Time:*** During the Easter preparation have a special worship service where each person explores his or her own caring responses to others. God cared for us so much that he gave his only Son. During the service each person could raise the questions: What am I giving in response to God's love and care? How much am I caring for others? How am I living a Christian life?

b. *Picnic for Graduating Seniors:* Early in the summer is a nice time to have a picnic. The entire church could hold a celebration for all the seniors graduating from high school. This event marks a new beginning for the young people. It is a time when the youth need the caring support of their church.

c. *The Church Finds Time to Play:* Plan a day for local church members to eat and play together—a picnic or an ice-cream social accompanied by games and contests. Have a variety of activities available so everyone can participate. Be particularly aware that the church consists of persons of all ages, including the very young and the older members.

WORSHIP

Caring can be greatly enhanced and motivated during times of worship. The remembrance, challenge, and dedication that can happen at these moments is best expressed in the way people care for one another. The following six activities suggest specific ways pastoral care concerns may be emphasized in the worship service. Some of the Creative Sharing Activities may also be adapted to the worship service.

a. *Worship service for analyzing one's problems:* As a creative way to help people analyze personal problems and/or specific sins that limit their growth, ask each to come to an informal session or campfire program to think about forgiveness and those problems in life most difficult for them. Provide each with one large nail, pencil, and one or more 3 x 5 cards. Persons are asked to write on the card(s) the problem that bothers them the most and limits their growth. Each card is folded several times while all participants are asked to think in silence about ridding their lives of the hindering attitude or activity. A wooden cross is then carried into the gathering. Hammers are made available and participants nail their folded papers onto the cross. Discuss together another 2,000-year-old cross which relates to forgiveness. The cross, with the sins and problems, is then burned as the group discusses forgiveness, overcoming evil with good, and the scripture, "Forgetting those things which are behind, I press on towards the mark...."

b. *Letters of appreciation:* In a caring community people are able to meaningfully touch the lives of one another. Plan a time when the members have the opportunity to write a letter to someone in the church through whom they experienced the Spirit of God in the past year. Writing such a letter can be a beautiful experience—almost as beautiful as receiving such a letter.

c. *Intergenerational worship services:* Plan one worship service each month which calls forth participation from persons of all ages. Scripture readings could be taken from some of the modern language translations of the Bible or from the Children's New Testament (which would have particular meaning to the younger members in the church family). Some texts which particularly cite the worth of children and youth are Matthew 18:1-4 IV (18:1-5 RSV), Mark 10:11-4 IV (10:13-16 RSV), Luke 18:16, I Timothy 4:12, and III Nephi 8:23-25. Church singing could include selections from *The Hymnal* and supplements, and music included in children's and youth church school resources. Persons of various ages could bear testimonies, read scriptures or other appropriate material, offer prayers, and contribute solos or ensemble music. Family groups might be asked in advance to prepare a "gift" of their individual and/or combined talents which would express their testimony of the Lord Jesus Christ. "Gifts" may include a brief drama, songs, poems, readings, art objects, handcrafts. Let this be an occasion of great joy as the church family celebrates its unity in Christ.

d. *A service of change and commitment:* A service of testimony and commitment could enable members of the church family to engage in a personal inventory for the purpose of selecting one specific personal change which would free them to express their discipleship in new ways. This service could be based on Matthew 19:20, "What lack I yet," or Philippians 3:13-14, "This one thing I do." Give worshipers a sheet of paper and a pencil. Ask them to fold the sheet in two, top to bottom. On the top half, invite them to write a response to one of the two scriptures suggested above. For example, a response could be written to one of these questions:

What are some of the important aspects of the Christian life which may be lacking in your life? If you could do one thing to more adequately express your discipleship, what would it be? Then, on the bottom half of the paper, worshipers may write one or several specific plans for gaining that which they said they lacked, or for carrying out the one thing they said they would like to do. If appropriate, verbal expressions of commitment could be received or prayers of support could be offered for the new decisions reached.

e. ***Contributing to the lives of others:*** Provide a worship experience in which each member lists three ways in which he/she can restore dignity and value to the lives of three other persons during the next six months. Name those people and set a date to accomplish each.

f. ***Committing gifts to God:*** Plan a worship experience centering on the gifts of each individual (Doctrine and Covenants 119:8b). Distribute slips of paper to participants. Audio and/or visual stimulation should be provided that reveals different people using their gifts in response to God's grace. Invite each person to write on the piece of paper a specific personal statement of commitment to God's work. Provide opportunity for all to stand and bring slips of paper as an offering to the rostrum or appropriate receiving point in the sanctuary. The act of getting up and moving to bring these offerings is an important part of the experience. Close the service with a hymn of dedication such as 379, "Take My Life and Let It Be Consecrated."

WEEKEND EVENTS

Occasionally one- or two-day events can bring a cohesiveness to relationships among persons that is more difficult to achieve in the one- or two-hour sessions. Here are suggestions to help in planning such weekend opportunities.

a. ***Caring through sharing work:*** Schedule a weekend workday at the local church building or at the homes of several elderly or disabled Saints for the purpose of performing needed maintenance work. Such events provide valuable opportunities for the Saints to share their gifts of time and talent in meaningful fellowship and ministry. These gatherings are appropriate in any season of the year.

b. ***Congregational renewal retreat:*** Sometimes the summer months are slow in local church life because families are on vacations and going to camps and reunions. A "renewal" weekend retreat may be just what church people need to create excitement and enthusiasm. This will give them an opportunity to get back in touch with each other. It will also provide time for them to meet new families or individuals who have started coming to church during the summer.

c. ***Learning about pastoral care:*** Plan to use the Pastoral Care Workshop Kit which will enable persons to understand, experience, and live pastoral care. It is designed to be presented by local leaders. The kit consists of suggested activities, resources, and all the directions necessary for a local leader to conduct the workshop. (God's promise will then be expressed through his people.) Order from the Pastoral Care Office, the Auditorium, Box 1059, Independence, MO 64051. Rental: $6.00.

d. *Using the Family Life Workshop Kit:* Caring relationships in the family don't just happen. They call for skills and practice. Set aside a time for several families to participate in a workshop together. Write to the World Church Pastoral Care Office for the Family Life Workshop Kit, Pastoral Care Office, the Auditorium, Box 1059, Independence, MO 64051. It is a planned workshop package which will be a rich resource for your church. Rental: $6.00.

AUDIOVISUAL RESOURCES

The Audio-Visual Resource Catalog may be purchased by sending your request and address and one dollar ($1.00) to   Audio-Visual Resource Library
Box 1059
Independence, MO 64051.

Many films and sound filmstrips available can help to motivate, train, or evoke a response in groups. Here are some suggested uses for a few films listed in the catalog.

a. *Film on caring for others:* Plan a service where the film, *Martin, the Cobbler*, is used. An excellent resource, it illustrates that people serve Christ by caring for one another. It is a 28-minute, color, 16mm film. Rental order F-71, cost $12.50. (Order

at least two to three weeks in advance, and include alternate showing dates.)
b. *Filmstrips exploring the value of self:* Structure a learning situation for children and/or adults in which concepts of inner beauty and the value of self are explored. Three sound filmstrips are suggested as resources: "The Velveteen Rabbit," SFS 127, 7½ min., $1.50; "Seeing Persons in People," SFS 156, 10 min., and "People Are Like Rainbows," SFS 576, 4 min., $1.50.
c. *Service on caring involvement:* Develop a service on caring involvement in the lives and well-being of others. The song "Looking for Space" by John Denver may be used...or perhaps the film "Cipher in the Snow" (F-26, 24 min., rental, $6.00).

SUMMARY

Planning for and using these activities can be a creative and rewarding venture. Look for settings already in the church program where these activities will enhance the existing ministry. Encourage small groups of two or three families to gather for informal fellowship in homes to share these activities together. Emphasis should be placed on getting to know one another better. Perhaps a potluck meal or light refreshments could be served. Communication activities, games, and singing might be included. One family might be designated to prepare a short worship experience which would be meaningful to all family members present, young and old. This would be an excellent opportunity to use some of the material from *Be Swift to*

Love by Barbara Howard or the *Family Enrichment Book* by Carol Anway and R. Daniel Fenn. Both are available from Herald House.

Pastoral care can be planned, and it can become a very meaningful part of the gathered and scattered ministry of the church. It is hoped that these activities are only the beginning of a search for ways to provide opportunities for people to experience knowing, caring, and communicating in the religious setting.

STUDY SUGGESTIONS

Spend time reading all the activities suggested in this chapter. Individually, as a family, or as a congregation, choose the activities you would like to experience. Begin planning the dates and settings for the activities you choose. May God bless your experiences together.

AUTHORS

HARRY J. ASHENHURST
Master of Divinity, M.A. in Counseling, Ph.D. candidate in Counseling Psychology, Director of Pastoral Care Office for the Reorganized Church of Jesus Christ of Latter Day Saints.

KAY SHERIDAN
M.A. in Counseling and Educational Psychology, Specialists degree in Family Therapy; she is presently doing therapy in a Substance Abuse Clinic in Mt. Pleasant, Michigan.

JOE A. SERIG
M.A. in Secondary Education, Ph.D. in Higher Education Administration and Community Leadership, Director of Program Planning Division for the Reorganized Church of Jesus Christ of Latter Day Saints.

S. LEE PFOHL
Master's candidate in Religion and Persons, Commissioner of the Outreach Commission for the Reorganized Church of Jesus Christ of Latter Day Saints.

IRENE JONES
B.A. in English Education, Staff Executive in the Christian Education Office for the Reorganized Church of Jesus Christ of Latter Day Saints.

PAT ZAHNIZER
M.A. in History, working on an M.A. in Learning Disabilities; presently teaches a learning disability class in Center Point, Iowa.

MYRON ANDES, JR.
M.A. student in Religion, Intern in the Pastoral Care Office from January 1979 to January 1980.

A. BRUCE LINDGREN
Master of Divinity, Director of Basic Leadership Curriculum in Temple School for the Reorganized Church of Jesus Christ of Latter Day Saints.

R. DANIEL FENN
Master of Divinity, M.A. in Counseling, Staff Executive in the Pastoral Care Office for the Reorganized Church of Jesus Christ of Latter Day Saints.

CAROL ANDERSON ANWAY
M.S. in Guidance and Counseling, Staff Executive in Christian Education for the Reorganized Church of Jesus Christ of Latter Day Saints.